Painless Police Report Writing

An English Guide for Criminal Justice Professionals

SECOND EDITION

BARBARA FRAZEE

JOSEPH N. DAVIS

PEARSON

Prentice
Hall

Upper Saddle River, New Jersey 07458

Library of Congress Cataloging-in-Publication Data

Frazee, Barbara.
  Painless police report writing: an English guide for criminal justice professionals/
  Barbara Frazee, Joseph N. Davis.—2nd ed.
    p. cm.
  Includes index
  ISBN 0-13-112324-6
    1. Police reports—Authorship. 2. English language—Rhetoric. 3. Report writing. I.
  Davis, Joseph N. II. Title.

HV7936.R53F73 2004
808'.066364—dc21   2003043382

Editor-in-Chief: Stephen Helba
Executive Editor: Frank Mortimer, Jr.
Assistant Editor: Sarah Holle
Marketing Manager: Tim Peyton
Editorial Assistant: Barbara Rosenberg
Managing Editor: Mary Carnis
Production Liaison: Brian Hyland
Production Editor: Janet Bolton
**Director of Manufacturing
  and Production:** Bruce Johnson
Manufacturing Manager: Ilene Sanford

Manufacturing Buyer: Cathleen Petersen
Creative Director: Cheryl Asherman
Cover Design Coordinator: Miguel Ortiz
Cover Design: Amy Rosen
Cover Art: Jeff Hayes, AFP/Corbis
Composition: The GTS Companies
Printing and Binding: Banta, Harrisonburg
Cover Printer: Phoenix Book Tech
Copyeditor/Proofreader: Maine Proofreading
  Services

Pearson Prentice Hall™ is a trademark of Pearson Education, Inc.
Pearson® is a registered trademark of Pearson plc
Prentice Hall® is a registered trademark of Pearson Education, Inc.

Pearson Education LTD.
Pearson Education Australia PTY, Limited
Pearson Education Singapore, Pte. Ltd.
Pearson Education North Asia Ltd.
Pearson Education Canada, Ltd.
Pearson Education de Mexico, S.A. de C.V.
Pearson Education—Japan
Pearson Education Malaysia, Pte. Ltd.
Pearson Education, Upper Saddle River, New Jersey

10 9 8 7 6 5 4 3

ISBN 0-13-112324-6

Contents

Preface

Legal charges may be filed or dismissed, court cases may be won or lost—all based on police officers' reports. Most law enforcement officers do not go into law enforcement because they love to write reports. When officers do encounter writing problems, often they do not know where to turn to find the solutions to these problems. Police academy report writing classes may be taught by law enforcement professionals without the English grammar to explain concepts and help struggling recruits. In desperation, frustrated officers turn to lower division and community college English composition classes.

Unfortunately, traditional English grammar and composition courses do not address many of the unique writing needs and requirements that go into a viable police narrative. Officers may come away from an English class with what, for them, may be useless terminology and overly involved or lengthy sentences—in short, a feeling that they have wasted their time. What now?

It was with these concerns in mind that the authors approached the writing of this text. They combined their talents and proven expertise in English instruction and police training to provide students and teachers with a reliable, relevant, and highly readable text. The result is an English text with law enforcement professionals in mind.

All the chapters have an introduction, stated objectives, explanatory text, and practice exercises geared specifically to police interests. At the end of each chapter, there is a chapter review, discussion questions, and review exercises, most in the form of police narratives, not isolated and unrelated sentences such as those found in many traditional grammar texts. In all examples, practices, and exercises, "deadwood words" have been replaced with "clear-meaning," everyday words such as those that should be used in clear, concise, well-written police narratives. Because the authors believe it is important to teach more than report writing and English in criminal justice programs and because they believe it is important to maintain equality as part of the educational process, every practice, exercise, or example includes all races and both genders in a variety of activities.

The first five chapters are devoted to presenting English grammar in a straightforward, easy-to-understand manner, using a conversational-style format. The last two chapters are devoted to the police report writing process. They include the types and uses of individual reports, interviewing and note-taking techniques and strategies, the organization of police reports, and proper word usage—in short, the rudiments of well-written police narratives.

A *Student Workbook* at the end of the text includes additional exercises to provide more practice for students who feel they want or need additional reinforcement. In addition, practice scenarios are provided that afford students an opportunity to put to use all the grammatical concepts and report writing techniques they have learned in the preceding chapters.

The *Instructor's Manual* includes answers to the 172 practice examples, 38 discussion questions, and 355 exercise examples. Special tips or suggestions are included at the beginning of each chapter review.

The entire text incorporates English grammar and composition skills with proven effective police report writing techniques and strategies. It emphasizes the importance of correct English composition for accurate police reports. Moreover, the unique combination of the authors' experience and background—an English instructor of more than twenty years with practical experience in police report writing needs and an active deputy sheriff and expert police trainer—guarantees a text that is relevant for today's law enforcement personnel as well as being a permanent personal resource and guide for English grammar and report writing techniques.

The authors wish to acknowledge the following reviewers: Wayne Coates, Pitt Community College, Greenville, NC; Clyde Cronkhite, Western Illinois University, Macomb, IL; Bill Elfo, Chief of Police, Blaine Police Department, Blaine, WA; David R. Graff, Kent State University-Tuscarawas, New Philadelphia, OH; Jeff Magers, SUNY College at Brockport, Brockport, NY; and Neal Strehlow, Fox Valley Technical College, Wautoma, WI.

1

Parts of Speech

INTRODUCTION

Words, which are the building blocks of language, are used in eight different ways. They have, therefore, eight different names, called the *parts of speech*. The work of each part of speech is to help build sentences. These parts of speech are nouns, pronouns, verbs, adjectives, adverbs, prepositions, conjunctions, and interjections. Below is a general definition for each part of speech. Usage of the parts of speech is covered in later chapters.

OBJECTIVE

At the end of this chapter, you will be able to identify the eight parts of speech.

NOUN

Look around the classroom and name the things that you see. All the objects that you have named are nouns. Many things that you associate with your classroom but that you cannot see or touch are also nouns: interest, thought, education, instruction, cooperation. These are abstract nouns. A noun is a name word; it is the name of something, something that you may or may not be able to see or touch.

Common Nouns

A common noun is any member of a class of persons, places, or things. These nouns are not capitalized.

> **Examples:**
> man, burglar, child, gold, city, police department

Proper Nouns

A proper noun is the name of a particular person, place, or thing. These nouns are capitalized.

> **Examples:**
> Mr. Johnson, Christopher, Christmas, Orange County Sheriff's Department, Santa Ana

Abstract Nouns

Abstract nouns are intangible concepts.

> **Examples:**
> justice, mercy, truth, honesty, knowledge, wisdom

Collective Nouns

A collective noun is a number of persons or things considered one group or whole.

> **Examples:**
> jury, crowd, mob, flock, team, herd

Learning Tip

In subject–verb agreement, a collective noun can be either singular or plural depending on whether the noun is considered a single unit or its members are considered individually. (See Chapter 2, "Subject–Verb Agreement.") If the collective noun remains a single unit, a singular verb is used.

> **Example:**
> The jury was deadlocked.

However, if the group has become divided and each member is considered separately, a plural verb is used.

Example:
The jury were from many parts of the city.

PRACTICE

Identify what type of nouns the following words are:

_____   police station

_____   morals

_____   Thanksgiving

_____   gloves

_____   committee

PRONOUN

A pronoun is a word that is used to take the place of a noun. *Pro* is a prefix that means *for;* therefore, pronoun means "for a noun." The pronoun gives the noun a rest. It may stand for the name of a person, place, thing, or idea.

Examples:
he, she, it, they, them, their, you, your, someone, anything

PRACTICE

Identify the pronouns in the following list of words:

_____   his

_____   we

_____   man

_____   her

_____   something

VERB

The verb is the part of speech that shows action or state of being. When verbs show state of being, they are called *linking verbs*. Verbs are the most important part of speech. The verb is one of the foundation words of a sentence. It gives the sentence meaning by saying something about the subject.

Examples:
hit, think, drive, catch, throw, search (action verbs)
is, are, was, were (linking verbs)

Learning Tip

Every sentence must contain a verb.

PRACTICE

Identify the verbs in the following list of words:

_____ run

_____ arrest

_____ shiny

_____ handcuff

_____ shoot

ADJECTIVE

Adjectives are words that modify, limit, or describe (affect the meaning of) the nouns or pronouns with which they are used. They explain "which one," "what kind of," or "how many."

Examples:
older, shiny, bright, pretty, dirty, many, few

PRACTICE

Identify the adjectives in the following list of words:

_____ intoxicated

_____ homely

_____ quickly

_____ new

_____ quiet

Articles

The words *a, an,* and *the* are special types of adjectives called *articles*.

ADVERB

Adverbs are words that tell manner (how), time (when), place (where), or degree (how much, to what extent) about other words. Adverbs modify (change the meaning of, limit, or describe) three parts of speech: verbs, adjectives, or adverbs. Often, but not always, adverbs end in *-ly*. Sometimes adverbs, such as *very* and *too*, are intensifiers.

Examples:
closely, quickly, very, soon

PRACTICE

Identify the adverbs in the following list of words:

_____   quietly

_____   ugly

_____   new

_____   wisely

_____   modestly

PREPOSITION

The preposition is a useful little word. It shows the relationship between a noun or pronoun and some other word in the sentence.

Examples:
to, in, on, between, among, with, near, of

Learning Tip

Most prepositions are "mouse" words; anything a mouse can do to a box is a preposition.

Examples:
The mouse can be *on* the box, *in* the box, *by* the box, or *near* the box.

PRACTICE

Identify the prepositions in the following list of words:

_____   from

_____   to

_____   at

_____   near

_____   lost

CONJUNCTION

The term conjunction comes from two Latin words: *con,* which means "together," and *jungere,* which means "join." A conjunction joins things together. In grammar, a conjunction is a word that joins one part of a sentence with another, one group of words with another, or simply one word with another.

Examples:
and, but, or, nor, for (coordinating)
when, although, since, however (subordinating)

PRACTICE

Identify the conjunctions in the following list of words:

_____ now

_____ for

_____ by

_____ but

_____ since

INTERJECTION

An interjection is a word or group of words that shows strong feeling or emotion. It usually comes at the beginning of a sentence and is set off by a comma or an exclamation point, depending on how strong the speaker's feeling is. An interjection has no grammatical relationship to the rest of the sentence. It is an independent word, not connected with the rest of the sentence.

Examples:
Hey, help, halt, hands up

PRACTICE

Identify the interjections in the following list of words:

_____ Hey you!

_____ Police!

_____ Stop or I'll shoot!

_____ Help!

_____ Open the door!

Learning Tip

The same word may be used as more than one part of speech. You cannot tell what part of speech a word is until you know how it is used in the sentence.

Examples:
He scored the winning *run* for the department softball team. (noun)
The officers usually *run* five miles every day. (verb)
It was a one-*run* ball game. (adjective)

CHAPTER REVIEW

The parts of speech are the building blocks of language and are used in eight different ways. The work of each part of speech is to help build sentences. You should know and be able to identify the eight parts of speech.

Nouns: name persons, places, things, ideas, or qualities (abstract nouns).
Pronouns: replace nouns.
Verbs: express (show) action or state of being (existence).
Adjectives: tell which one, what kind of, or how many about nouns and pronouns.
Adverbs: tell when, where, how, how much, or to what extent about verbs, adjectives, and other adverbs.
Prepositions: show relationship between noun or pronoun and some other word in the sentence. Most of them are "mouse" words—anything a mouse can do to a box.
Conjunctions: join words, phrases, or clauses.
Interjections: show strong feeling.

DISCUSSION QUESTIONS

1. What are the eight parts of speech?
2. Is a word always the same part of speech in every sentence? Use the word *patrol* to explain your answer.

EXERCISES

In each of the following sentences, underline and identify the part of speech requested.

1. Adverbs
   Yesterday, Mrs. Sanchez was walking home alone.

2. Pronouns
   Mrs. Sanchez said she didn't know who had stolen her purse.

3. Conjunction
   The officers talked to Mrs. Sanchez and searched the area.

4. Prepositions
   The officers found two of the suspects in the warehouse near the scene of the crime.

5. Interjections
   The officers yelled, "Hey! What are you two doing in the warehouse?"

6. Verbs
   The officers arrested two of the suspects and searched for the third.

7. Nouns
   Officer Washington found the third suspect standing in the crowd.

8. Adjectives
   The frightened victim identified the three suspects.

Identify all parts of speech in the following two sentences:

1. Officer Washington asked the three men to tell the truth.

2. The three men complained bitterly to District Attorney Hanson that the jury had violated their rights.

2

Sentence Elements

INTRODUCTION

In Chapter One, you learned to identify the parts of speech. In this chapter, you will learn how these parts of speech go together to form sentences. The elements of a sentence go together to make a complete thought. These elements include subjects, predicates, direct and indirect objects, subject complements, and modifiers.

OBJECTIVES

At the end of this chapter, you will be able to do the following:

1. Identify complete sentences.
2. Identify and correct fragments and run-on sentences.
3. Identify subjects and predicates.
4. Identify subject–verb agreement and regular and irregular verb forms and tenses.
5. Identify direct and indirect objects.
6. Identify subject complements and modifiers.
7. Identify phrases and clauses.

COMPLETE SENTENCE

A sentence is a group of words containing a subject and a verb and expressing a complete thought. It is the basic unit in any writing. There are four basic types of sentences: simple, compound, complex, and compound–complex.

Simple Sentences

A simple sentence contains only one main (independent) clause. A clause is a group of words that contains a subject and a predicate.

> **Example:**
> The officer wrote the citation.

Compound Sentences

A compound sentence contains two or more main clauses, but no subordinate (dependent) clauses.

> **Example:**
> You may not catch the suspect, but you should try.

Complex Sentences

A complex sentence has one main clause and one or more subordinate clauses.

> **Example:**
> If the suspect hits tonight, we'll be ready.

Compound–Complex Sentences

A compound–complex sentence has two or more main clauses and one or more subordinate clauses.

> **Example:**
> If the suspect hits tonight, you go in front, and I'll cover the rear.

FRAGMENT

A fragment is a group of words that is punctuated as a sentence but does not contain a main clause (complete thought). Frequently, a fragment is incorrectly punctuated as a sentence.

> **Examples:**
> Knowing I'd find narcotics. (incorrect)
> I searched the house, knowing I'd find narcotics. (correct)

RUN-ON SENTENCE

A run-on sentence is also referred to as a "fused" sentence. A run-on sentence combines two or more independent clauses without punctuation or a coordinating conjunction.

Examples:

The officer collected all the evidence he arrested the suspect. (incorrect)

The officer collected all the evidence. He arrested the suspect. (correct)

The officer collected all the evidence and arrested the suspect. (correct)

The officer collected all the evidence, and he arrested the suspect. (correct)

PRACTICE

Label the following groups of words as complete (C), fragment (F), or run-on (R):

_____ The suspect left.

_____ The officer stopped the car he wrote a citation.

_____ Begin at the beginning.

_____ A male white, 6'2", blond hair.

_____ The trunk was searched, but it was empty.

SUBJECT

The subject is the part of a sentence about which something is stated. It is a word or group of words about which an assertion is made.

Example:

That division of the department has its work cut out for it.

Simple Subjects

The simple subject is the principal, main, or essential part of the complete subject.

Example:

That *division* of the department has its work cut out for it.

Complete Subjects

The complete subject is the simple subject and all its modifiers.

Example:

That division of the department has its work cut out for it.

Compound Subjects

A subject that consists of two or more simple subjects is called a compound subject.

> **Example:**
> *Training* and practical *experience* are both important.

Implied Subjects

Sometimes the subject of a sentence is not expressed. This is usually the case in an imperative or command sentence.

> **Example:**
> Write the citation. (*You*) write the citation.

Delayed Subjects

Sometimes an expletive or extra word is used to introduce a sentence. This extra word is not the subject.

> **Example:**
> *There* was only one prisoner in the cell. (Subject: prisoner)

PRACTICE

Underline the complete subject and circle the simple subject in the following sentences:

> My partner and I saw the driver run the stop sign.
>
> I turned on the overhead emergency lights, and the suspect stopped.
>
> I walked up to the driver's door, and my partner went to the passenger's door.
>
> The man in the driver's seat had a foreign passport in his hand.
>
> He was an ambassador to the United Nations.

PREDICATE

The predicate of a sentence tells what is stated about the subject. The verb, that is, the simple predicate, in a sentence makes a statement about what the subject is or what the subject does.

Simple Predicates

The simple predicate is a verb or verb phrase. A verb phrase is the main verb plus any helping verbs.

Examples:
That division of the department *has* its work cut out for it. (verb)
That division of the department *will have* its work cut out for it. (verb phrase)

Complete Predicates

The complete predicate is the verb or verb phrase and all its modifiers.

Example:
That division of the department *has its work cut out for it.*

Nonaction Verbs (Predicates)

Some words are verbs even though they show no action. They can be used alone or with other words, both action and nonaction, as helping or auxiliary verbs.

Examples:
The suspect *was* tall.
The traffic violator *became* obnoxious.
The suspect *can run* fast.
They *had been drinking* for two hours.

There is a complete list of nonaction/linking verbs at the end of the text.

Compound Predicates

A compound predicate consists of two or more verbs or verb phrases.

Example:
The party goers *watched, yelled,* and *threw* bottles.

Learning Tip

Both subjects and predicates can be compound.

Example:
The watch commander or the captain will arrive and give the briefing.

PRACTICE

Underline the complete predicates and circle the verbs in the following sentences:

My partner and I saw the driver run the stop sign.

I turned on the overhead emergency lights, and the suspect stopped.

I walked up to the driver's door, and my partner went to the passenger's door.

The man in the driver's seat had a foreign passport in his hand.

He was an ambassador to the United Nations.

SUBJECT–VERB AGREEMENT

The subject of a sentence must agree with its verb in number. Singular subjects require singular verbs, and plural subjects require plural verbs.

Examples:
The driver looks like the suspect. (singular)
The drivers look like the suspects. (plural)
The officer was on patrol. (singular)
The officers were on patrol. (plural)

Generally, subject–verb agreement poses no problem for the police report writer; however, there are several exceptions, which are discussed below.

Intervening Prepositional Phrases

An intervening prepositional phrase is a group of words that starts with a preposition, ends with a noun, and comes between the subject and the verb.

Example:
The new ammunition *for the revolvers* works well.

The subject is *ammunition*, and the verb is *works*. The prepositional phrase, *for the revolvers*, is an adjective and modifies ammunition.

Learning Tip

The exception to this rule is when the subject is *none, some, most,* or *all*. When this occurs, the intervening prepositional phrase determines subjects–verb agreement.

Examples:
Some of the revolvers were missing.
Some of the ammunition works well.
All of the evidence was booked.
All of the items were booked.

Other Intervening Phrases

These phrases are groups of words that come between the subject and the verb and, if removed from the sentence, would not change the meaning of the sentence.

Examples:

The sergeant, *along with four officers*, was at the scene.

Certain things in life, *especially a good arrest record*, make him happy.

The defendant, but not his two friends, was arrested. (negative expression)

Collective Nouns

A collective noun names a group as a single unit.

Examples:

jury, mob, crowd, team, squad, detail

When a collective noun is used as a group, the verb must be singular. When the individual members of a collective noun act separately, the verb must be plural.

Examples:

The jury reached its decision. (group, therefore singular)

The jury were asked their opinions on the case. (individuals, therefore plural)

Measurements

When times, hours, monetary amounts, lengths, or measurements are used as subjects and considered as a unit, the verb must be singular.

Example:

Forty hours is a full week's work.

Either...Or/Neither...Nor(Compound Conjunctions)

When *"either...or/neither...nor"* contains both a singular and plural noun and is used as the subject, the word close to the verb determines agreement.

Examples:

Neither the chief nor his *captains* were at the meeting. (plural)

Neither the captains nor the *chief* was at the meeting. (singular)

Special Words

The following words look plural but are singular: economics, news, ethics, politics, mathematics, measles, whereabouts, physics.

The following words may seem to be singular but are plural: scissors, pliers, acoustics, trousers.

Learning Tip

If you are unsure if a word is singular or plural, check the dictionary.

PRACTICE

Circle the correct form of the verbs in the parentheses:

One of the victims (was/were) not sure she could identify the suspect.

All of the boxes of ammunition (has/have) been accounted for.

New developments in crime scene investigation techniques (mean/means) better evidence recovery.

The chief, but not his captains, (was/were) at the meeting.

The jury (has/have) reached a unanimous decision.

Either the boys or their father (was/were) lying.

Neither the prime suspect nor his accomplices (was/were) admitting anything.

A pair of gloves (was/were) the only evidence.

The scissors (seem/seems) to be the murder weapon.

Most of the group of perspective jurors (is/are) present.

IRREGULAR VERBS

Regular verbs form the past tense by adding -d or -ed to the root or base word. Irregular verbs, on the other hand, change their spelling in their principal parts.

Examples:
look–looked, sneak–sneaked, cite–cited (regular verbs)
write–wrote, drink–drank, drive–drove (irregular verbs)

The simple past tense forms have no helping verbs whether the main verb is regular or irregular.

Examples:
She looked outside.
They heard a suspicious sound.
He drove the prisoner to jail.

Past participle forms follow helping verbs such as *has, have,* and *had.*

Examples:
She has looked outside.
They have heard a suspicious sound.
He had driven the prisoner to jail.

Learning Tip

Of is never a helping verb. You may say, "He could *of* done it."
What you should say, and must write, is "He could *have* done it."

Some irregular verbs can be troublesome if the writer forgets what each verb means.
Hang, meaning to hang an object from a hook or from the wall:

Examples:
He *hangs* the picture.
He *hung* it yesterday.
He *has hung* it.

Hang, meaning to hang a person by a rope around the neck:

Examples:
The prisoner *hangs* today.
He *hanged* yesterday.
He was *hanged* at dawn.

Lie, meaning to lie down, to recline:

Examples:
He *lies* down.
He *lay* down yesterday.
He *had lain* in bed for two days.

Lay, meaning to put or place:

Examples:
She *lays* her books on the table.
She *laid* them down.
She *has laid* them there before.

Raise, meaning to lift something:

Examples:
The attorney *raises* victims' hopes.
The attorney *raised* their hopes.
The attorney *had raised* their hopes.

Rise, meaning to lift oneself, to ascend or get up:

Examples:
He *rises* at 0600 hours every morning.
He *rose* late yesterday.
He *has risen* late several mornings this week.

Sit, meaning to use a chair, to be seated:

Examples:
She *sits* there.
She *sat* there yesterday.
She *has sat* there before.

Set, meaning to put or place something:

Examples:
He *set* the gun on the table.
He *set* it there yesterday.
He *had set* it there before.

Shine, meaning to give light:

Examples:
The light *shines* in his eyes.
The officer *shone* the flashlight in the window.
The police *had shone* their spotlight on the suspect.

Shine, meaning to polish:

Examples:
The recruits *shine* their shoes every morning.
They *shined* them twice.
They *have shined* them every day for weeks.

See the complete list of irregular verbs at the end of the text.

VERB TENSES

All the verbs in a sentence need to be in the same tense or time frame when possible.

Examples:
He gathered the evidence, tagged the items, and logs them into the evidence book. (incorrect)
He gathered the evidence, tagged the items, and logged them into the evidence book. (correct)

PRACTICE

In the space provided, write the correct past tense form of the verb given in parentheses:

The captain had (give) _____ us instructions and (show) _____ us what to do.

That police station was (build) _____ fifty years ago.

Mrs. Meyers said she had (drive) _____ the car only one month when it was (steal) _____.

Officer Ramirez (do) _____ a good job on her last assignment.

The burglar was (go) _____ before the sleepy residents (see) _____ him.

DIRECT OBJECT

A direct object is the noun or pronoun that comes after an action verb. It is the word that tells who or what receives the direct action of that verb.

Example:
The inmate washed the *car*.

INDIRECT OBJECT

An indirect object is always a noun or pronoun that comes between the action verb and the direct object. It is a word that answers the question "to or for what" or "to or for whom" the action of the sentence was done. However, the words "to" and "for" do not appear in connection with an indirect object, and an indirect object can never be a prepositional phrase. To have an indirect object, the sentence must have an action verb and usually a direct object.

An indirect object is used after verbs such as *give, buy, pay, grant, sell, send, promise, show,* and *tell* and other words that express the idea of telling, or transferring something to another.

Examples:
He gave the *driver* a ticket. (indirect object)
He gave a ticket *to the driver*. (prepositional phrase)

Learning Tip

Using indirect objects in place of prepositional phrases will shorten police narratives.

SUBJECT COMPLEMENTS

Subject complements come in two varieties: predicate nouns and predicate adjectives.

Predicate Nouns

A predicate noun is a noun or pronoun that comes after a linking verb. It renames or means the same thing as the subject.

Example:
He is the *captain* of the Investigation Division.

Predicate Adjectives

A predicate adjective is an adjective that comes after a linking verb. It describes or tells something about the subject.

Examples:
She was *tired.*
The man looked *suspicious*.

PRACTICE

Underline the direct objects and/or subject complements in the following sentences; circle any indirect object you may find:

The ballistics department matched the bullets.

Many of the people appeared surprised at the outcome of the trial.

Unknowingly, Mr. Tweed sold them some stolen merchandise.

The suspect magically undid the handcuffs and amazed the spectators.

She was the only female officer in the department.

Learning Tip

Sentences cannot contain both direct objects and subject complements because these two sentence elements follow different kinds of verbs.

MODIFIERS

Modifiers explain, describe, or limit some other word in a sentence and should be placed, in most cases, as close to that word as possible. Modifiers can be single words or groups of words. As you learned in Chapter One, adjectives and adverbs are two kinds of single-word modifiers.

Adjectives

Adjectives modify, describe, or limit nouns, pronouns, and other adjectives. They answer the questions which one, what kind of, and how many.

Examples:
older, shiny, bright, pretty, dirty, many, few

PRACTICE

Identify the adjectives in the following list of words:

_____ disoriented

_____ several

_____ slowly

_____ wise

_____ noisy

Adverbs

Adverbs modify, describe, or limit verbs, adjectives, and other adverbs. They answer the questions when, where, how, how much, and to what extent. Many adverbs end in -*ly*, and many of these are formed by adding -*ly* to an adjective: *real* to *really*. Some adverbs have two forms, one with -*ly* and one without: close, closely.

Examples:
closely, quickly, very, soon

PRACTICE

Identify the adverbs in the following list of words:

_____ softly

_____ often

_____ clear

_____ reckless

_____ promptly

Three Forms of Adjectives and Adverbs

Adjectives and adverbs have three forms: positive, comparative, and superlative.

When you make a statement, you use the positive form.

Example:
He is strong.

When you compare two people or things, you use the comparative form.

Example:
He is stronger than Bob.

When you compare three or more people or things, you use the superlative form.

Example:
He is the strongest of all the officers.

Learning Tip

Good and *well* are both adjectives. The difference between "I feel good" and "I feel well" is a difference of meaning, not grammar. *Good* means a state of happiness; it is also used after such linking verbs as *be, taste, smell, become, look, seem,* and *sound. Well* means that a person does not feel ill or that he is in good health or healthy. *Well* can also be an adverb as in "He ran well."

Phrases

Groups of words used as modifiers are either phrases or clauses. Phrases are groups of related words that do not contain a verb and its subject and are used as a single part of speech. The two most common phrases are prepositional phrases and participial phrases.

Prepositional Phrases.   A prepositional phrase is a group of words that begins with a preposition and ends with a noun or pronoun. These phrases can act as either adjective or adverb modifiers, depending on what word the phrase is describing.

Prepositions are words that show relationships between nouns and other words; they can be particularly tricky in technical writing. In describing a crime scene, you might have to write about something being *near, next to, against,* or *by* something else. Using the wrong preposition can create the wrong word picture in your report.

Examples:
That store *on the corner* opened yesterday. (adjective)
That store opened *on the corner* yesterday. (adverb)

Participial Phrases.   These function just like one-word adjectives do, except that they are word groups and are made by a *verbal,* which is a word formed from a verb but not used as a verb, plus modifiers or complements. Participial phrases may be either present or past tense.

Examples:

Present Tense

The van *waiting at the corner* was the getaway vehicle.
Standing on the corner, Deputy Smith saw the entire accident.
Mr. Mason, *waiting for the light to change,* saw the bus as it approached.

Past Tense

Injured in the accident, Betty was unable to go to work for a month.
The woman *injured in the accident* was unconscious when they took her to the hospital.
Betty, *injured in the accident,* will be off work for a month.

PRACTICE

Underline the prepositional or participial phrases in the following sentences:

The gun was ncxt to the body.

The marijuana was in the car.

The suspect said, "You can find the body in the trunk."

The suspect, arrested at the scene, did not waive his rights.

Arrested at the scene, the suspect admitted he had the gun.

Clauses

Unlike phrases, clauses are groups of related words that usually contain a subject and a verb. There are two kinds of clauses: *independent* (also called main or principal) and *dependent* (also called subordinate). An independent clause can stand alone as a complete sentence, but a dependent clause cannot.

Examples:

He succeeded in bringing the criminal to justice. (independent clause)

...although it had taken long hours of intense investigation. (dependent clause)

Dependent clauses can be used as adjectives or adverbs.

Examples:

Adjective

Someone *who knew the combination* had to open the vault.

Adverb

The suspect left *when he saw the patrol car.*

Learning Tip

Think of the "p" in phrase as meaning "part of a sentence" and the "c" in clause as meaning "a complete sentence." Thus a phrase is not a complete sentence, and a clause is a complete sentence.

Misplaced Modifiers

Although misplaced modifiers, those that are not placed close to the word they describe, can often be humorous, they can also be very embarrassing and give an inaccurate account of events in a police report.

Examples:

The officer only found two suspects. (incorrect)

The officer found only two suspects. (correct)

I had been driving for forty years when I fell asleep at the wheel and hit a tree. (incorrect)

I had been driving for forty years without an accident. Last night I fell asleep while driving and hit a tree. (correct)

Dangling Modifiers

Dangling modifiers are words or groups of words that do not modify another word or phrase or that cannot be easily linked to the sentence.

Examples:

After running six blocks, the car left as the suspect reached it. (incorrect)

After the suspect ran six blocks, the car left as he reached it. (correct)

PRACTICE

Underline the misplaced/dangling modifiers in the following sentences:

Soon after crossing the border, my stomach sickness got better.

John sold the car to a friend with a bent fender.

Still giggling, the elevator took us to the eleventh floor.

Just walking along, my shoelace broke.

Foaming at the mouth, the dog warden had the stray put to sleep.

Parallelism

Parallelism is the use of structures that are grammatically similar. Sentences must be parallel: words must be balanced with words, phrases with phrases, dependent clauses with dependent clauses, and so forth. When you use nonparallel constructions in your sentences, those sentences sound awkward.

Examples:

His speech was about law enforcement, gun control, and that crime is increasing. (incorrect)

His speech was about law enforcement, gun control, and crime rates. (correct)

CHAPTER REVIEW

Sentences may be simple, compound, complex, or compound–complex. When a group of words is punctuated as a sentence but does not contain a complete thought, that group of words is called a fragment. When two or more independent clauses are written together as one sentence without proper punctuation or without a coordinating conjunction, that sentence is called a run-on or fused sentence.

The main elements of a sentence are the subject and predicate. The complete subject is the simple subject and all its modifiers. The complete predicate is the verb or verb phrase and all its modifiers. The subject and verb in a sentence must agree in number: singular subjects take singular verbs; plural subjects take plural verbs. Intervening phrases generally have no bearing on subject–verb agreement.

Verbs are either regular or irregular. Regular verbs form their past tense by adding -d or -ed to the root word. Irregular verbs change their spelling in the past tense and past participle.

Direct objects follow action verbs and receive the direct action of those verbs. Indirect objects come between action verbs and direct objects. They tell to or for whom the action was done.

Subject complements follow linking verbs and come in two varieties: predicate nouns and predicate adjectives.

Modifiers may be single words or groups of words. These groups of words are called phrases and clauses. A phrase is not a complete thought. A clause, on the other hand, is a complete thought and may be dependent or independent.

Misplaced/dangling modifiers are those words or groups of words that are not placed close to the words they describe. Misplaced/dangling modifiers can give the reader an inaccurate or unclear account of events in police reports.

All sentences must be written with parallel constructions: like grammatical structures must be joined to like grammatical structures.

DISCUSSION QUESTIONS

1. What are the four types of sentences?
2. What are the two main elements of a sentence?
3. What is another word for the simple predicate?
4. How do regular and irregular verbs differ? Give an example of each.
5. What sentence elements come after action verbs?
6. What sentence elements come after linking verbs?
7. What are modifiers? Can they be single words or groups of words?
8. What are the groups of words used as modifiers called?
9. What is the difference between phrases and clauses?
10. What are misplaced/dangling modifiers?

EXERCISES

Label the following sentences as complete (C), fragment (F), or run-on (R). Correct fragments and run-ons.

_____ 1. Mr. Gold left his office at lunch he went to the bank and got money out of the ATM machine to go to the health club.

_____

_____

_____ 2. He didn't see anyone near the ATM when he arrived at the bank.

_____

_____

_____ 3. After he got the money.

_____

_____

Underline the complete subject and circle the simple subject in the following sentences.

1. Unaware of the suspect, Gold took his money and left.

2. The suspect, dressed in black, stepped out from behind the bushes.

Underline the complete predicate and circle the verb or verb phrase in the following sentences.

1. The suspect pulled a handgun out of his pocket and pointed it at Gold.

2. The suspect quietly demanded all of Gold's money.

Underline the simple subject once and the verb twice. Watch for intervening phrases.

1. Gold said, "No."

2. The suspect, along with Gold, didn't see the witness run to the phone.

Choose the correct forms of the verbs in the following sentences.

1. Gold and the suspect (was/were) the only people left on the street.

2. When Gold refused to give the suspect any money, the suspect (swung/swang) at Gold with the gun.

Underline the direct object and/or subject complements in the following sentences; circle any indirect objects you may find.

1. Gold was afraid for his life.

2. He gave the suspect his money.

Locate and underline the misplaced or dangling modifiers in the following sentences. Correct the errors. In some cases, you may have to rewrite the sentences.

1. The suspect ran down the street carrying Gold's money.

   _____

   _____

2. The witness said he'd called the police yelling to Gold.

   _____

   _____

Revise the following sentences so they use parallel constructions.

1. The police arrived, questioned Gold, and were beginning to search the area.

   _____

   _____

2. Gold described the suspect as being tall, wearing black clothes, with brown curly hair, and dark eyes.

   _____

   _____

Rewrite the following sentences and correct all grammatical errors.

1. The witness was also able to describe the suspect the same as Gold is describing except the witness wasn't close enough to see the suspect's eyes.

   _____

   _____

2. Officer Carver seen the suspect running through the park still carrying the gun.

   _____

   _____

3. Officer Frick and his partner Officer Frack caught the suspect at the corner of Fifth and Main.

   _____

   _____

3

Pronouns

INTRODUCTION

Pronouns, one of the eight parts of speech mentioned in Chapter One, are words used in place of nouns. Generally, pronouns are used to refer to nouns that have already been used or implied. These nouns or noun phrases, called *antecedents,* appear before or shortly after the pronouns. Using pronouns shortens your writing and makes it less tedious and repetitious.

OBJECTIVES

At the end of this chapter, you will be able to do the following:

1. Identify and use pronouns correctly.
2. Write and/or correct sentences using clear antecedents.
3. Write and/or correct sentences containing pronouns with regard to number, case, gender, and person.

TYPES OF PRONOUNS

Pronouns can be divided into several main classes.

Personal Pronouns

Personal pronouns can be either singular or plural.

> *Singular*: I, you, he, she, it
> *Plural*: we, you, they

They can also be used as subjects, as in the list above, or as objects: me, you, him, her, us, you, them.

Example:
The Chief told the officers *he* was reassigning *them.*
                           (subject)   *(object)*

Possessive Pronouns

Possessive pronouns are used to show ownership. Like personal pronouns, possessive pronouns can be either singular or plural. They may also act as adjectives.

> *Singular*: my, mine, your, yours, his, her, hers, its
> *Plural*: our, ours, your, yours, their, theirs

Examples:
It was *her* car that was stolen.
The stolen car was *hers.*

Learning Tip

Unlike nouns, which use apostrophes to show possession, pronouns never use apostrophes to show possession.

Examples:
The guns were Nathan's and Ben's.
The guns were theirs.

Indefinite Pronouns

An indefinite pronoun does not refer to a specific person or thing. Therefore, it has no specific antecedent.

Some indefinite pronouns are always singular and take a singular verb.

Examples:
another, anybody, anyone, anything, each, either, everybody, everyone, much, neither, nobody, no one, nothing, one, somebody, someone, something
Everyone was on time.

Learning Tip

The indefinite pronouns listed above also take singular pronouns if they are acting as antecedents.

Example:
Everyone had his gun.

Some indefinite pronouns are always plural and take a plural verb.

Examples:
both, few, many, several, others
Both of the men were guilty.

Exception: Rarely, *many* is used as a singular pronoun.

Example:
Many a criminal finds his life spent in jail.

Some indefinite pronouns can be either singular or plural, depending on the antecedent.

Examples:
all, any, most, none, some
All of the ammunition was accounted for.
All of the guns were loaded.

Interrogative Pronouns

Interrogative pronouns are used when asking questions.

Examples:
who, whom, whose, which, what
What did the deputy say?
Whose gun did he use?

Relative Pronouns

Relative pronouns are used to connect a group of words to some other word or group of words in a sentence.

Examples:
which, who, whose, that, whom, and compounds such as whoever
The gun that Gunther used was a Walther.

Learning Tip

Generally, *who, whose, and whom* are used when the antecedent is a person. *Which* is used when the antecedent is a thing or object. *That* can be used in either case. Also, use *who* and *whoever* when the pronoun is a subject.

Examples:
Who was the suspect?
Whoever knows the victim's name should call the police.

Use *whom* and *whomever* when the pronoun is an object or when the pronoun precedes an infinitive (*to* plus a verb).

Examples:
Whom did you see enter the bank?
To *whom* did you give the information?
Call *whomever* you wish to testify.

Use *whose* when the pronoun is a possessor.

Example:
The police are searching for the person *whose* letter threatened the judge's life.

Demonstrative Pronouns

Demonstrative pronouns point out specific persons, places, and/or things for special attention. They can be singular or plural.

Singular: this, that
Plural: these, those

Examples:
This is the woman who kidnapped the child.
Those are the items the police took from the suspect.

Demonstrative pronouns can also be used as adjectives.

Example:
This woman kidnapped the baby.

Reflexive/Intensive Pronouns

Reflexive/intensive pronouns are formed by adding the suffix *-self* or *-selves* to some personal pronouns. They can be either singular or plural.

Singular: myself, yourself, himself, herself, itself
Plural: ourselves, yourselves, themselves

These pronouns are used to show an action affecting the one who performs it (reflexive) or to show emphasis (intensive).

Examples:
Reflexive: The Chief called the meeting *himself.*
Intensive: The Chief *himself* called the meeting.

PRACTICE

Underline the pronouns in the following sentences:

They robbed the bank yesterday.

The thieves stole their car last night.

Mrs. Chen said someone must have seen what happened.

Who could identify the suspect?

The lieutenant asked whichever officers were available to volunteer for extra duty.

These were the only items missing from the house: a VCR, two radios, and a diamond ring.

The burglar himself left the only clue.

AGREEMENT

Pronouns should agree with their antecedents in number, case, gender, and person.

Number

If an antecedent is singular, then the pronoun must be singular. Likewise, if the antecedent is plural, the pronoun must be plural.

Examples:
The suspect released *his* hostages. (singular)
The suspects released *their* hostages. (plural)

Two or more nouns or pronouns joined by *and* are plural.

Example:
Officers Kelly and Hogan aimed *their* guns at the suspects.

When two nouns are joined by *or* or *nor,* the pronoun normally agrees with the second noun.

Examples:
Either the boys *or* their father was guilty.
Neither the man *nor* his sons were hurt.

A noun or pronoun followed by a prepositional phrase is treated as if the prepositional phrase were not there.

> **Examples:**
> Three *suspects* in the holdup ran to *their* car.
> The *book* of matches had no identification on *its* cover.

Case

Pronouns must agree with their antecedents in case. If a pronoun replaces a subject noun, the pronoun must be in the subjective case.

> **Examples:**
> *Deputy Sparling* received a letter of commendation.
> *She* saved several children's lives.

If a pronoun replaces an object noun, such as a direct or indirect object or an object of a preposition, the pronoun must be in the objective case.

> **Examples:**
> The teller gave *Sgt. Kim* a description of the suspect.
> The teller gave *him* a description of the suspect.

Learning Tip

When a noun and a pronoun are used together or when two pronouns are used together, you may find yourself trying to decide whether to use the subjective or objective case pronoun. Simply read the sentence with each pronoun by itself; you should be able to tell by the sound of the sentence which pronoun form is correct.

> **Examples:**
> The victim gave Sgt. Seaver and *I or me* the suspect's description.
> The victim gave *me* the suspect's description.

Gender

Pronouns should agree with their antecedent in gender: masculine or feminine. Not long ago it was acceptable to say, "A police officer should consider all *his* options before *he* acts." Today, however, many people object to sentences that imply that all officers are male, which is not the case. To eliminate sexism in your writing, you can edit your sentences in several ways.

You can use the double-pronoun construction, which is widely accepted today.

> **Example:**
> A police officer should consider all his or her options before he or she acts.

As you can see, if repeated, double pronouns become tedious.

Another option is to make both the antecedent and the pronoun plural.

Example:

Police officers should consider all *their* options before *they* act.

A third option is to eliminate all reference to specific gender. This is a particularly good option when you can use it.

Example:

A police officer should consider all options before acting.

Person

Pronouns in the same sentence must agree in person with each other.

Examples:

One can live happily in an area if *you* feel *you* have good protection.
(incorrect)

One can live happily in an area if *he/she* feels *he/she* has good protection.
(correct)

You can live happily in an area if *you* feel *you* have good protection.
(correct)

PRONOUN REFERENCE

Pronouns must not only agree with their antecedents, but those antecedents must also be clearly recognizable or referred to. Most problems that occur with pronouns can be traced back to unclear pronoun references: which antecedent is the pronoun referring to or replacing?

Example:

If the police dog won't eat its food, try covering it with warm gravy.

The pronoun *it* has no clear antecedent; it could refer to either the dog or the food. Logically, you would want *it* to refer to the food.

Example:

If the police dog won't eat its food, try covering the food with warm gravy.

Sometimes the only way to correct an unclear pronoun reference is to repeat the antecedent and eliminate the pronoun.

PRACTICE

Circle the correct pronouns in parentheses in the following sentences:

Officer Pickens said (him/he) and his canine partner worked well together.

The Chief left the discussion up to (we/us) officers.

The store owner gave the description to Officer Stein and (I/me).

The new position will be offered to either you or (I/me).

Each of the suspects wanted to answer the charges for (themselves/herself).

CHAPTER REVIEW

Pronouns are useful words that take the place of nouns. The nouns or noun phrases that pronouns replace are called antecedents. Pronouns can be classified under several categories. Pronouns must have clear antecedents and must agree with these antecedents in number, case, gender, and person.

DISCUSSION QUESTIONS

1. What is a pronoun?
2. What is an antecedent?
3. List the main types of pronouns, and give examples of each type.
4. Pronouns must agree with their antecedents in what four ways?

EXERCISES

Underline the pronouns in the following sentences.

1. The officer asked, "Who called the police?"

2. The victim said, "I called. Someone stole my car."

3. The officer asked, "Could someone you know have taken it?"

4. "I told my family whoever needed it could take the car."

Select the correct pronoun in the following sentences.

1. Do you think one of *they/them* took it?

2. Neither of the girls has *her/their* license.

3. My wife and *me/myself/I* don't think the girls took it.

Circle and correct the pronoun problems in the following sentences.

1. The officer told the victim he didn't have enough information.

   _____

   _____

2. The officer told the victim if he intends to file a report, you'll have to be more helpful.

   _____

   _____

3. He said if he got more information he could call later.

   _____

   _____

Correctly punctuated police reports are clear and understandable, helping you provide clear and accurate testimony.

4

Mechanics

INTRODUCTION

The mechanics of English grammar include capitalization, punctuation, and writing numbers. While these mechanics may not seem important to you in writing police reports, they are. Correct capitalization shows where sentences begin and identifies proper nouns. Punctuation includes the correct usage of periods, commas, colons, and the like. Correctly written numbers eliminate errors.

OBJECTIVES

At the end of this chapter, you will be able to do the following:

1. Use capital letters correctly.
2. Punctuate sentences correctly.
3. Write numbers correctly.

CAPITALIZATION

In the following instances, you would commonly use capital letters in police reports. If you block print your reports, capital letters must be larger than the other letters.

First Words

Capitalize the first word in a sentence, in a direct quotation, and in a line of regular poetry.

> **Examples:**
> He is the new officer.
> The sergeant said, "Welcome to the department."
> We're all happy you are here.
> After work, join us for a beer.

Proper Nouns

The first letter of a proper noun is capitalized. The pronoun *I* is always capitalized.

People, Organizations, and Their Members.

> **Examples:**
> Walter James
> Tulsa Police Department
> Captain Walter James

Places and Geographical Areas.

> **Examples:**
> New York City
> New England
> the South, West, North, East, Midwest, Southwest

Learning Tip

Do not capitalize directions.

> **Example:**
> The speeding vehicle turned *east* on Main Street.

Rivers, Lakes, and Mountains.

> **Examples:**
> Rio Grande River
> Lake Superior
> Mt. Rushmore

Ships, Airplanes, Trains, and Space Vehicles.

Examples:

Queen Mary

Concorde

Union Pacific

Discovery

Nationalities, Races, Tribes, Languages, Religions, and Political Parties.

Examples:

Canadian

Caucasian

Navajo

Spanish

Methodist

Democratic

Family Relationships. Capitalize words that indicate family relationships when they are used in place of a person's name.

Examples:

We asked Dad if we could go.

We asked our dad if we could go.

Titles.

Examples:

General Eisenhower

Dr. Stanley Fine, M.D.

Learning Tip

President, Presidential, Presidency, and Executive are capitalized when they refer to the office of the President of the United States. The same format is followed for the Vice President.

Deity and the Bible. Capitalize the words Bible and Biblical when they refer to scripture.

Examples:

God, Jehovah, Allah

Brand Names and Registered Trademarks.

Examples:

Levis

Coors

Books, Publications, Magazines, Newspapers, Poems, Articles, Headings of Chapters, Plays, Television Shows, Songs, Paintings, and Other Works of Art. Capitalize the first word and all important words in titles of all the examples listed above.

Examples:
The Choirboys
Time, Los Angeles Times
Miracle on 34th Street

Days, Months, Holidays, and Holy Days.

Example:
Thursday, November 25th is Thanksgiving.

Courts.

Example:
the Supreme Court

Historical Events, Documents, and Time Periods.

Examples:
the Great Depression
the Bill of Rights
the Middle Ages

Adjectives Formed from Proper Nouns. You capitalize the adjective, but not the noun that follows it.

Examples:
German shepherd
French restaurant

Names of the Seasons. Capitalize them only when they refer to specific seasons of specific years.

Examples:
The Winter of 1840 was the worst on record.
This winter has been very mild.

Correspondence. You capitalize the salutation and the first word in the complimentary closing of a letter.

Examples:
Dear Carl,
Sincerely yours,

PRACTICE

Correct all capitalization errors in the following sentences:

sergeant Davis said, "merry christmas."

On Christmas Day, the Sergeant said, "Merry Christmas."

Are you leaving on thursday to go back east for the Holidays?

No, father Flannigan mailed my present to my Aunt's.

i think it's a book about mississippi river boats.

PUNCTUATION

Punctuation marks are to a reader what road signs are to a driver. They make it easier to understand what a person has written.

Periods

You use periods with abbreviations after a statement, a command, a request, an indirect question and at the end of a sentence.

> **Examples:**
> Mr. and Mrs. Roger Perez, Jr.
> Blvd.
> Babe Ruth started his career as a pitcher.
> Sit down and be quiet.
> Stop where you are.
> He asked if she could identify the suspect.

Question Marks

You use question marks after a direct question.

> **Example:**
> Did anyone see what happened?

Exclamation Marks

You use exclamation marks to give emphasis or to show strong feeling to a word, phrase, or sentence. Use exclamation marks only when you are quoting someone; officers cannot add their own emphasis.

> **Example:**
> Drop the gun!

PRACTICE

Add the end punctuation marks as needed in the following sentences:

Maple Ave. is the correct street

Go there and wait

He asked if she saw anyone

Did you see anybody

Let me out of here

Commas

You use commas to separate or set apart elements within a sentence.

Items in a Series.   You use commas to separate items in a series of three or more when the items are separated by *and* or *or*. There is always a comma before the conjunction.

Example:
The thief took the money, two lamps, and the washing machine.

Compound Sentences.   You use commas to separate the clauses of a compound sentence that are connected by a coordinating conjunction.

Example:
He admitted he was guilty, but he pleaded for mercy.

Parenthetical Phrases.   You use commas to set off parenthetical expressions, words not necessary to the meaning of the sentence.

Example:
The witness, you say, is gone.

Nouns of Direct Address.   You use commas to set off a noun of direct address. A noun of direct address identifies the person you are talking to.

Example:
Sergeant Adams, have you identified the suspect?

Appositives (Explanatory Equivalents).   You use commas to set off appositives. Appositives are nouns or noun phrases that rename or explain the noun.

Example:
Mr. C. M. McCreedy, our police chief, is at a meeting.

Dates.   You use commas to separate the day of the week from the month, the month from the year, and the date of the month from the year. You use a comma after the last part of the date if the sentence continues.

Examples:
Monday, January 24, 1945
January, 1945
On January 24, 1945, Secret Service agents arrested Brown.

Addresses.   You use commas to set off the name of a building or business from the street address, the street address from the city, the city from the state, but not the state from the zip code. Use a comma after the last part of the address if the sentence continues.

Examples:
Tomaine Tommy's Bar
1000 South Retch Street
Your Town, CA 00001

Tomaine Tommy's Bar, 1000 South Retch Street, Your Town, CA 00001

I'll meet you at Tomaine Tommy's Bar, 1000 South Retch Street, Your Town, CA 00001, after dinner.

Introductory Clauses and Phrases.   You use commas after introductory adverb clauses, verbal phrases to set off *yes* and *no* and other explanatory words and phrases.

Examples:
If you see a crime in progress, call the police. (adverb clause)
Before taking the stand, the witness conferred with her lawyer. (adverb phrase)
Putting down his gun, the suspect surrendered. (verbal)
No, he won't be in court.
In my opinion, he was innocent. (introductory prepositional phrase)

Learning Tip

If the adverb clause is at the end of the sentence, you do not usually set it off with a comma.

Example:
Call the police if you see a crime in progress.

Nonrestrictive Clauses and Phrases.   You use commas to set off a clause or phrase that, if eliminated, would not change the meaning of the sentence.

Example:
The suspect, who had a gun in his hand, said, "Gimme the money."

Direct Quotes.   You use commas to set off short quotations and sayings that are the speaker's exact words. End commas go inside the quotation marks.

Examples:

The suspect said, "Gimme the money."

She's a real "swinger," no doubt, but somewhat disorganized.

Contrasted Elements.   You use commas to set off contrasting parts of a sentence.

Example:

He is ill, not drunk.

Titles and Degrees.   You use commas to separate names from titles, degrees, or similar information.

Examples:

Samuel T. Arnold, Jr.

William E. Carey, M.D.

Ronald D. Stuart, Sergeant, New York Police Department

Correspondence.   You use commas after the salutation in a personal or friendly letter and after the closing of a letter.

Examples:

Dear Carl,

Sincerely yours,

For Clearness.   You use a comma to set off any elements of a sentence that might be confused or misunderstood.

Example:

Where she was, was no concern of mine.

Adverbial Conjunction.   You use a comma after an adverbial conjunction that joins the independent clauses in a compound sentence.

Example:

The chief of police was unable to speak at the banquet; consequently, another speaker took his place.

PRACTICE

Insert commas where necessary in the following sentences:

After baking mother did the laundry.

While painting my sister accidentally broke a window.

The officer saw them slide scramble and tumble down the embankment.

In his pocket the suspect had a switchblade a vial of a white powdery substance about a yard of nylon string and a roach clip.

Gentlemen this is Don Duefuss the new investigator.

The prosecuting attorney asked "This is the weapon found at the scene is it not?"

Sherlock Holmes met Dr. Watson in front of 22 B Baker Street London England on January 1 1901.

They couldn't decide whether to look further or radio for assistance.

Jack the Ripper the infamous criminal was never arrested.

Semicolons

You use a semicolon between independent clauses not joined by a coordinating conjunction. In an earlier chapter, you learned that two independent clauses form a compound sentence.

Example:
The chief of police was unable to speak at the banquet; another speaker took his place.

You use semicolons between elements in a list of three or more when there are commas in the elements.

Example:
Officer Dugan arrested Letty Evans, a shoplifter; Sally Adams, a street-walker; and Rebecca Irving, a con-artist.

You use semicolons before conjunctive adverbs connecting two independent clauses. Examples of conjunctive adverbs are *therefore, however,* and *nevertheless.*

Example:
The officers arrived at the scene; however, the burglars had already left.

Colons

You use colons in the following instances.

Business Letter Salutation. You use a colon after the salutation in a business letter.

Examples:
Dear Sergeant Garcia:
To Whom It May Concern:

Formal Quotation.   You use a colon to introduce a formal quotation.

Example:

The chief began his talk with these words: "It is a great pleasure to be here tonight."

Introducing Listings (List of Appositives).   You use a colon after a complete statement introducing a list.

Example:

The evidence technician collected the following: fingerprints, photographs, and a handgun.

Explanations.   You use a colon after a statement followed by a closely related explanation.

Example:

The new pursuit policy serves two purposes: it protects the public and the officers.

Times.   You use a colon between numbers showing hours and minutes.

Example:

The meeting is at 10:30 A.M.

Ratios.   You use a colon between numbers in a ratio.

Example:

The City Council questioned the officer-to-population ratio of 1:1,000.

Divisions of Plays and the Bible.   You use a colon between the act and scene of a play and between the chapter and verse in Biblical passages.

Examples:

A famous speech in Shakespeare's plays is in *Richard III,* 1:1. Sometimes fans bring signs to the game that read, "John 3:16."

PRACTICE

Add semicolons and colons to the following sentences:

The sergeant missed briefing another officer took his place.

The rookie officer questioned Sam Spade, the shop owner Helen Montgomery, the customer and Maria Jimenez, the landlord.

The combination and handle had been knocked off however, the thieves hadn't had time to finish getting into the safe.

At 430 P.M. the suspect took the following items a gun, a ring, and a box of ammunition.

The FBI crime statistics are divided into two parts Part I and Part II crimes.

Apostrophes

You use apostrophes to form contractions, plurals in some cases, and to show possession.

Contractions. You use an apostrophe to form a contraction: a shortened form of two words or a date. The apostrophe takes the place of the missing letter(s) or number(s).

> **Examples:**
> couldn't (could not)
> can't (cannot)
> won't (will not)
> Class of '52 (Class of 1952)

Plurals. You use an apostrophe to show plurals of symbols, numerals, letters used as letters, and words that usually do not have plurals.

> **Examples:**
> Mississippi is spelled with four *s*'s, four *i*'s, and two *p*'s.
> There were too many *that*'s in his report.

Possessives. Possessives show ownership. You use an apostrophe to show the possessive of singular and plural nouns and group names and to indicate the amount of time, space, or quantity. The rules to form possessives are as follows.

Singular possessives. Add ('s) to all nouns, whether they end in *s* or not.

> **Examples:**
> victim's jewels
> James's gun

Plural possessive. Add (') to plural nouns ending in *s*.

> **Examples:**
> suspects' gun
> victims' rights

Add ('s) to plural nouns not ending in *s*.

Examples:

gentlemen's agreement

children's toys

Group names.   Add ('s) to the final word in a group name.

Example:

Drug Enforcement Bureau's report

Time, Space, and Quantity.   Add ('s) to show the amount of time, space, or quantity.

Examples:

five minutes' work

one hour's time

two miles' distance

two dollars' difference

Quotation Marks

You use quotation marks in the following instances.

Double Quotation Marks. You use double quotation marks to enclose the exact words of a speaker; to enclose titles of stories, articles, chapters, short poems, and songs; and to enclose unfamiliar words, slang, or jargon.

Examples:

The sergeant said, "Felony arrests are up this month. You're doing a good job."

"The Lottery" (short story)

"The Charge of the Light Brigade" (poem)

"God Bless America" (song)

I've heard him called "loony" and "oddball."

Learning Tip

You usually place punctuation inside end quotation marks.

Example:

The suspect said, "I give up."

Exception: You place question marks outside end quotation marks when the question is not a part of the quoted portion.

Example:

Did Pam say, "You must go"?

Single Quotation Marks.   You use single quotation marks when a quotation comes inside another quotation.

Examples:
The teller said, "The suspect said, 'Gimme the money.' "
The suspect said, "Come and get me 'cop'er'!"

PRACTICE

Add apostrophes and quotation marks to the following:

Hurry! Weve only got two minutes until the bank closes.

Why did he capitalize all of the *buts* in his report?

Nine officers guns were missing from the womens locker room.

The officer said, They were all taken in one hours time.

Hyphens

You use hyphens in the following instances.

Words and Parts of Words. You use hyphens to link words and parts of words.

Examples:
door-to-door search
pro-police

Numbers and Fractions. You use hyphens to link numbers and fractions.

Examples:
twenty-one through ninety-nine
one-half

Word Divisions. You use hyphens to divide words at the end of a line. Remember to divide words only at syllable divisions.

Example:
The officer arrested the suspect for auto theft.

Dash

You use a dash (—) in the following instances.

Summarize Statements. You use a dash before a summarizing statement such as "these" or "all."

Example:
Patrol officers, motorcycle officers, and sergeants—these officers were all at the riot.

Repeated Expressions. You use a dash to emphasize a repeated expression.

Example:

He is the victim—the only victim of the crime.

Change in Thought. You use a dash to indicate an abrupt change in thought.

Example:

I had originally planned—but that's too long a story.

Missing Letters. You use a dash to show missing letters in confidential correspondence.

Example:

The memo is for Captain F—.

Interrupter. You use a dash to set off parenthetical expressions that make abrupt interruptions.

Example:

About once a month—sometimes oftener—there is a bomb scare.

Dates and Numbers. You use a dash in place of *to* in dates and numbers.

Examples:

He was chief, 1967–79.
Read pages 55–89.

PRACTICE

Add hyphens and dashes to the following:

A three year prison sentence is not enough for that crime.

One third of the crimes in small towns are committed by juveniles.

Johnny G is the name of the juvenile suspect.

Bloods and Crips these were the gangs at the meeting.

Ralph Emerson was in prison from 1845 48.

Parentheses

You use parentheses in the following instances.

Numbers or Letters in a Series. You use parentheses around numbers or letters that mark items in a series.

Example:

He gave three field sobriety tests: (1) finger dexterity, (2) spelling, (3) balance.

Explanation or Side Remark.   You use parentheses around an explanation or side remark.

Example:

Deputy Karr (what an appropriate name) works auto theft.

References, Directions, and Sources of Information.

Example:

Gang homicides increased 10% (LAPD).

Translation.   You use parentheses to enclose the translation of a phrase.

Example:

The officer arrested Mr. Baldwin for deuce (driving under the influence).

Spelled-out Numbers.   You use parentheses to enclose figures to ensure accuracy.

Example:

The suspect took forty dollars ($40).

Underlining

You use underlining in the following instances.

Titles.   You use underlining for titles of books, magazines, newspapers, pamphlets, movies, radio and TV programs, plays and long poems; plane, train, and ship names; and works of art. These would be italicized in printing.

Example:

The Choirboys

Words, Letters, or Numbers.   You use underlining for words, letters, or numbers used as words. It is also correct to use quotation marks in these instances.

Example:

There is no z in surprise.

Ellipses

An ellipsis is an omission in a direct quotation. You use three or four periods to show ellipses. You use three periods in the middle of a quotation, and you use four periods at the end of a sentence or between two sentences.

Examples:

Highway Patrol Commander Kelly said, "You've done a good job...so keep up the good work."

Kelly also said, "The Department has overcome great obstacles...."

Learning Tip

Avoid using ellipses whenever possible because it shows you have intentionally left out part of a quotation. You may be required in courtroom testimony to explain why you intentionally omitted statements. The defense attorney may try to use your decision, use of an ellipse, against you to attack your credibility.

PRACTICE

Add parentheses, underlining, and periods (for ellipses) in the following:

The new pursuit policy has three provisions: 1 speed limits, 2 number of cars, and 3 supervisor's responsibilities.

Dr. Bones what a great name for the pathologist did the autopsy.

The hype a heroin addict was under the influence.

The captain said, "and he won't be back."

The victim paid twenty dollars $20 for her copy of The Onion Fields.

NUMBERS

You either spell out or use numbers in the following instances.

Sentence Beginnings

You spell out numbers at the beginning of a sentence.

Example:

Forty officers voted in favor of the raise.

Ages

You use figures only when ages are stated in years, months, and days; otherwise, write out the age.

Examples:
The child was 5 years, 2 months, and 20 days old.
The department is seventy-five years old.

Decimals and Percentages

You write out decimals and percentages at the beginning of a sentence; otherwise, you use figures.

Examples:
Thirty percent of the applicants passed.
The average score is 30 percent.

Long Numbers

You use figures and commas to show numbers of four or more digits.

Example:
57,908

Measurements and Capacities

You use figures for measurements and capacities.

Examples:
23 gal.
150 lb.
15 ft.

Military Groups or Units, Political Divisions, and Sessions of Congress

You spell out military groups or units, political divisions, and sessions of Congress.

Examples:
the One Hundred and First Air Borne
the Fourth Congressional District
the Eighty-second Congress

Money

You use figures for definite sums of money.

Example:
$445.78

You spell out indefinite sums of money.

Example:
The suspect took approximately fifty dollars.

PRACTICE

Select the correct usage of numbers in the following:

3/Three victims came to the station.

The youngest was 21/twenty-one years old.

One victim was missing exactly $23/twenty-three dollars.

The other was missing approximately $30/thirty dollars.

The police car took 18/eighteen gals. of gasoline.

CHAPTER REVIEW

You have learned the mechanics of English grammar, including capitalization, punctuation, and writing numbers. Correct capitalization shows where sentences begin and identifies proper nouns. Punctuation includes correct usage of periods, commas, colons, and the like. Correctly written numbers eliminate errors.

DISCUSSION QUESTIONS

1. When do you use capital letters?
2. What are the end punctuation marks, and when are they used?
3. Fifteen uses of commas were discussed in the chapter. Name five and explain them.
4. Explain the usage of semicolons and give one example.
5. Explain the usage of colons and give two examples.
6. Explain the three uses of apostrophes and give examples of each.
7. Explain apostrophe usage in forming possessives and give examples of each.
8. Explain how hyphens are used to divide words.
9. Define the term ellipsis and explain why caution is necessary in its use.
10. When do you write out numbers, and when do you use numerals?

EXERCISES

Correct the capitalization and number errors in the following sentences. Add correct punctuation where necessary.

1. Mrs Wood called the police department to report a Burglary.

2. She said, I've been robbed

3. Officer allen arrived at 230 to take the report

4. He asked her, "What happened"

5. She told him the following

6. She left the house at 9:00 A.M. and went to the store then to the gas station and finally to the Cleaners.

7. when she got home she found the front door open.

8. When she went inside the house had been ransacked the living room furniture was overturned.

9. She said the following items were missing 1 a copy of Gone with the Wind 2 her twenty one year old daughters address book and 3 one gal. of wine.

10. She wasnt sure, but thought the total loss was approximately $450.

5

Spelling

INTRODUCTION

Accurate spelling is essential in police report writing. Your spelling errors can confuse the reader and change the meaning of your report. Spelling errors can also make you look less competent than you are. In this chapter, you will learn some of the rules of spelling to help you correctly spell common words that may cause you trouble.

OBJECTIVES

At the end of this chapter, you will be able to do the following:

1. Spell words correctly.
2. Add prefixes and suffixes correctly.
3. Form plurals correctly.
4. Identify seven resources to aid you in correct spelling.

RULES OF SPELLING

Since there are many exceptions in English spelling, no one set of spelling rules will cover all cases. When you are in doubt, use a dictionary. However, the following rules will help you in many situations.

ie *or* ei

When the sound is long *ee*, use *i* before *e*, except after *c*. Remember the old folk rhyme that says:

Use *i* before *e* (e.g., believe, field, piece)
Except after *c* (e.g., receive, ceiling, deceive)
Or when sounded like *a*
As in *neighbor* and *weigh*. (e.g., freight, reign)

Learning Tip

There are ten exceptions to the above rule. It would be helpful for you to memorize them.

Exceptions: either, neither, leisure, seize, weird, foreign, height, counterfeit, forfeit, science

Prefixes

A prefix consists of one or more letters added before the root word to make a new word. You do not have to worry about single or double letters; simply write the prefix and add the root word as it is normally spelled.

Examples:

Prefix	*Root Word*	*New Word*
un	known	unknown
un	necessary	unnecessary
mis	spelled	misspelled

Suffixes

Suffixes are one or more syllables added after the root word. Unfortunately, adding a suffix is not as simple as adding a prefix.

Final Silent e. When adding a suffix to the word, you drop the final silent *e* if the suffix begins with a vowel (*a, e, i, o, u*).

Examples:

Root Word	*Suffix*	*New Word*
come	ing	coming
imagine	ary	imaginary
berate	ed	berated

Learning Tip

Exceptions: When the letter before the silent *e* is *c* or *g*, the word must keep the silent *e*; otherwise, the *c* (sounding like *s*) will change to the sound of *k*. Or the *g* (sounding like *j*) will change to the sound of "guh" as in *good*.

Examples:

noticeable, serviceable, peaceable

vengeance, courage, advantageous

The silent *e* is also kept in some cases to avoid confusion with other words: *singing* versus *singeing*. Unfortunately, many of these words do not follow a consistent pattern.

Examples:

change	-able	changeable
allege	-ing	alleging

Therefore, for words ending in *ce* or *ge*, you should check a dictionary.

When adding a suffix to a word, keep the silent *e* if the suffix begins with a consonant.

Examples:

Root Word	Suffix	New Word
hope	ful	hopeful
late	ly	lately
shame	less	shameless
close	ness	closeness

Learning Tip

Exceptions: Awful, argument, ninth, truly, wholly, duly, probably

Three common words have alternate spellings: abridgment/abridgement, acknowledgment/acknowledgement, judgment/judgement.

---

y *to* i

You change the *y* to *i* when you add a suffix preceded by a consonant. The exceptions are adding *-ing* or *-ist*.

Examples:

Root Word	Suffix	New Word
happy	ness	happiness
party	es	parties
try	ed	tried

Root Word	Suffix	New Word
study	ing	studying
copy	ist	copyist

When adding a suffix to a word that ends in -*y*, keep the *y* if the letter before the *y* is a vowel.

Examples:

Root Word	Suffix	New Word
valley	s	valleys
attorney	s	attorneys
deploy	ed	deployed

Exceptions: Some words ending in -*ay* are exceptions. There isn't any rule to identify them. When in doubt, you should check the dictionary.

Examples:

lay/laid, pay/paid, say/said, day/daily

Most verbs ending in -*ie* are exceptions to the change *y* to *i* rule. In verbs such as lie and die, you change the -*ie* to -*y* before adding -*ing*.

Examples:

lie/lying, die/dying

Final Consonants.   When a word ends in a consonant, sometimes the consonant is doubled and sometimes it is not when you add a suffix.

Double Consonants.   When the following conditions are present, you double the final consonant.

You are adding a suffix that begins with a vowel.

Examples:

-ing, -ed, -er, -est, -ist, -able
run*ning*, skip*ped*

The word to which you are adding the suffix is only one syllable, or if it has more than one syllable, the accent is on the final syllable.

Examples:

be*gin*, oc*cur*, com*pel*
begin*ning*, occur*ring*, compel*ling*

The word's last two letters must be one vowel and one consonant.

Examples:

commit + ed = committed, stop + ing = stopping

When adding -*ly* to a word ending in -*l*, keep the final *l*.

Examples:

careful + ly = carefully, brutal + ly = brutally

When adding *-ness* to a root word ending in *-n*, keep the final *n*.

Examples:
open + ness = openness, green + ness = greenness

Not Double Consonants. When the following conditions are present, you do not double the final consonant.

When the word ends in two or more consonants.

Examples:
jump + ed = jumped, find + ing = finding

When two or more vowels precede the final consonant.

Examples:
contain + ing = containing, appear + ed = appeared

When the word ends in a single accented vowel and a consonant and the suffix begins with a consonant.

Examples:
regret + ful = regretful, equip + ment = equipment

If the accent is not on the last syllable of the root word.

Examples:
quarrel + ing = quarreling, bigot + ed = bigoted

Plurals

You make singular nouns plural using several different spelling guidelines.

Adding -s. You add *-s* to make most nouns plural.

Examples:
books, automobiles, guns, suspects

Adding -es. You add *-es* to nouns ending in *s*, *ch*, *sh*, *x*, or *z*.

Examples:
Joneses, boxes, flashes, churches, inches, buzzes

Words Ending in -o. When words end in the letter *o*, use *-s* if a vowel comes before the final *-o*. If a consonant comes before the final *-o*, use *-es*.

Examples:
radios, scenarios, studios
heroes, potatoes, vetoes

Learning Tip

There are four exceptions: memos, pros, pianos, solos.

Words Ending in -f or -fe. For some words ending in *-f* or *-fe*, you change the *f* to *v* and add *-s* or *-es*. Some words don't change the *f* to *v*; just add *-s*.

Examples:
knife/knives, wife/wives, chief/chiefs, staff/staffs

Irregular Plurals. Some nouns have irregular plurals.

Examples:
foot/feet, child/children, man/men, woman/women

Unchanged Nouns. Some nouns do not change when you form the plural.

Examples:
sheep, moose, series, species

Compound Word. You make the last part of the compound word plural when the word is not hyphenated or written as two separate words. When they are written as two separate words or hyphenated, you make the most important part of the word plural.

Examples:
briefcases, mailboxes, brothers-in-law, bus stops

Learning Tip

Simple plural forms *never* have an apostrophe (') before the *-s* ending.

Examples:
Two boys left. (correct)
Two boy's left. (incorrect)

Seed Words

Words ending with the *seed* sound are usually spelled *-cede.*

Examples:
concede, intercede, precede, accede

There are only four exceptions: supersede, exceed, proceed, and succeed.

WORDS COMMONLY MISSPELLED IN POLICE REPORTS

abduction	accident
accelerated	accommodate
accessories	achievement

acquire
acquitted
affidavit
altercation
among
apparatus
apparent
arguing
argument
arson
assault
belief
believe
beneficial
benefitted
bureau
burglary
category
coercion
coming
commission
comparative
complainant
conscious
conspiracy
controversial
controversy
conviction
corpse
counterfeit
criminal
defendant
define
definitely
definition
describe
description
disastrous
dispatched
disposition
drunkenness
effect
embarrass
embezzlement
emergency
environment
evidence
exaggerate
existence
existent

experience
explanation
extortion
fascinate
forcible
fraudulent
height
homicide
indict
interest
interrogate
intimidation
intoxication
investigation
its (it's)
juvenile
larceny
led
legal
lieutenant
lose
losing
marriage
marshal
mere
necessary
occasion
occurred
occurrence
occurring
offense
official
opinion
opportunity
paid
particular
patrolling
pedestrian
penalize
performance
personal
personnel
possession
possible
practical
precede
precinct
prejudice
premises
prepare

prevalent	strangulation
principal	studying
principle	subpoena
privilege	succeed
probably	succession
procedure	suicide
proceed	summons
profession	surprise
professor	surrender
prominent	surveillance
prosecute	suspect
prostitution	suspicion
pursue	techniques
pursuit	testimony
quiet	than
receive	their
receiving	then
recommend	there
referring	they're
repetition	thieves
resistance	thorough
rhythm	to/too/two
robbery	traffic
sabotage	transferred
scene	trespassing
seize	truancy
sense	unnecessary
sentence	vagrancy
separate	victim
separation	villain
sergeant	warrant
serious	woman
sheriff	write
shining	writing
similar	written
statute	

HOMONYMS

Homonyms are words that sound alike but have different meanings and are spelled differently. You should learn the difference and use the correctly spelled word.

beat/beet	capital/capitol
boar/bore	ceiling/sealing
board/bored	cent/sent/scent
bread/bred	cereal/serial
break/brake	chord/cord
bridal/bridle	cite/sight/site
buy/by/bye	corps/corpse

Your spelling errors can confuse the reader and change the meaning of your report.

council/counsel/consul
current/currant
dear/deer
hole/whole
idle/idol
its/it's
knew/new
knot/not
know/no
lain/lane
lessen/lesson
liable/libel
lie/lye
loan/lone
made/maid
maybe/may be
meat/meet
medal/meddle
muscle/mussel
naval/navel
oar/or/ore
ordinance/ordnance
pail/pale
pain/pane
pair/pare/pear
pause/paws
peace/piece
peal/peel

pedal/peddle
peer/pier
plain/plane
pray/prey
presence/presents
pride/pried
principal/principle
rain/reign/rein
raise/rays/raze
rap/wrap
real/reel
right/rite/write
road/rode/rowed
role/roll
sail/sale
scene/seen
seam/seem
sense/cents
serf/surf
shear/sheer
shone/shown
soar/sore
sole/soul
stairs/stares
stake/steak
stationary/stationery
steal/steel
straight/strait

example	ex.
executive	exec.
federal	fed.
general broadcast	GB
government	govt.
headquarters	hdq.
highway	hwy.
hospital	hosp.
identification	ID
informant	inf.
inspector	insp.
junction	junc.
junior	jr.
juvenile	juv.
last known address	LKA
left	L
left front	LF
left hand	LH
left rear	LR
license	lic.
Lieutenant	Lt.
Lieutenant Colonel	Lt. Col.
location of birth	LOB
Major	Maj.
manager	mgr.
maximum	max.
medium	med.
memorandum	memo
middle initial	MI
misdemeanor	misd.
modus operandi	MO
National Auto Theft Bureau	NATB
National Crime Information Center	NCIC
no further description	NFD
no middle name	NMN
northbound	N/B
not applicable	NA
number	no.
numbers	nos.
officer/official	ofc.
Ohio driver's license (NMDL, FDL, etc.)	ODL
opposite	opp.
organization	org.
package	pkg.
page	p.
pages	pp.
passenger	pass.
permanent/personal identification number	PIN
pieces	pcs.
pint	pt.

place	Pl.
place/point of entry	POE
point of impact	POI
police officer/probation officer	PO
quantity	qty.
quart	qt.
received	recd.
required/requisition	req.
right	R
right front	RF
right rear/rural route/railroad	RR
road	Rd.
school	sch.
section	sect.
Sergeant	Sgt.
serial	ser.
southbound	S/B
subject	subj.
Superintendent	Supt.
surface	sur.
symbol	sym.
tablespoon	tbsp.
technical	tech.
teletype	TT
transportation	tran.
treasurer	trcas.
university	univ.
unknown	unk.
vehicle identification number	VIN
veterinarian/veteran	vet.
village	vil.
volume	vol.
weapon	wpn.
wholesale	whsle.

TIPS

The following seven tips should help you improve your spelling:

Speller's Journal: When you get a report back with misspelled words, write those words (correctly spelled) in the back of your notebook. You use the same words over and over, and soon you will correctly spell those words.

Dictionary: When in doubt, always use a dictionary to verify spelling and meaning.

Speller/Divider: Speller/dividers are pocket-sized books that list the words correctly spelled. They don't have any definitions. Most officers know what a word means but may not know how to spell it.

Thesaurus: A thesaurus is a book of synonyms, words with similar meanings. Use by police officers improves spelling and makes reports more interesting. It also helps you find a word with the exact meaning you need.

Misspeller's Dictionary: If you have trouble finding correctly spelled words in a dictionary, try a *Misspeller's Dictionary*. The words are listed incorrectly spelled, followed by the correct spelling, for example, *newmonia/pneumonia*.

Electronic Speller: Handheld, battery-powered electronic spellers are available. The more sophisticated models include a dictionary and thesaurus. They will correctly spell a word, but may not differentiate between homonyms.

Proofreading: Proofread your own work, or have someone read it for you. Proofreading will greatly reduce spelling errors.

CHAPTER REVIEW

You have learned that accurate spelling is essential in police report writing. You learned some of the rules of spelling to help you correctly spell common words that may cause you trouble. You also learned the importance of correctly using homonyms and abbreviations.

DISCUSSION QUESTIONS

1. What is a homonym?
2. How can homonyms cause trouble in your reports?
3. What are some of the resources you can use to check your spelling?

EXERCISES

Add the suffixes -*ed* and -*ing* to the following words.

1. raid _____

2. prevent _____

3. describe _____

4. rob _____

5. try _____

6. identify _____

7. study _____

8. die _____

9. allege   _____

10. hope   _____

Add *-able* to the following words.

1. rely   _____

2. note   _____

3. remark   _____

4. work   _____

5. excite   _____

Write the plural form of the following words.

1. officer   _____

2. witness   _____

3. child   _____

4. man   _____

5. attorney   _____

6. knife   _____

7. party   _____

8. box   _____

9. radio   _____

10. shelf   _____

Circle the correctly spelled words from the choices you are given.

1. accellerated	excelerated	accelerated
2. all right	allright	alright
3. burglary	burglery	berglary
4. dialated	dilated	diliated
5. homocide	homicide	homacide
6. lisence	license	licence
7. preceeded	preceded	precceeded

8. sargent   sergent   sergeant

9. secratery   secretary   secretery

10. warrent   warrant   warent

Circle the correct homonym in parentheses.

1. If the suspect walks down that (aisle, isle, I'll), I'll meet her at the front of the theater.

2. Reporters should not be (allowed, aloud) to leak information before a trial.

3. Smith refused to pay the (fair, fare) because she said the amount wasn't (fair, fare).

4. Officers found the jewel-encrusted (idle, idol) in the suspect's closet.

5. The (knew, new) recruit said he (knew, new) some of the local ordinances.

6. The witness was very (pail, pale).

7. He (passed, past, pasted) the detour because he drove right (passed, past, pasted) it.

8. This time, the detective obtained the (right, writ, write) (right, writ, write) so the judge didn't have to (right, writ, write) another.

9. The defense attorneys were unable to save (their, there, they're) client because (their, there, they're) wasn't evidence to refute the charges.

10. She said the (vial, vile) man had thrown the (vial, vile) of acid at her.

6

Police Reports

INTRODUCTION

The previous chapters provided you with English composition skills. In this chapter, you will learn about the different types of police reports, how they are used, and what makes a good report. Remember, the television and movie glamour of police work seldom includes report writing.

OBJECTIVES

At the end of this chapter, you will be able to do the following:

1. Define what a report is.
2. Identify the types of reports.
3. Define the uses and purposes of reports.
4. Define the qualities of a good report.

DEFINITION OF A REPORT

Traditionally, a report meant a "police report," or the narrative you have to write after completing an investigation. But, actually, reports take many different forms. A report is defined as the following: any documentation recorded on a departmental form, or other approved medium (computer disks), and maintained as a permanent record.

TYPES OF REPORTS

The following types of reports are commonly used in police departments across the United States. The titles of these reports may change from region to region, but the content and uses are the same.

Arrest Reports

Arrest reports are used to document the events that occur when you arrest a suspect. Many officers take little pride in or time and energy to complete arrest reports, yet the arrest report is one of the most important reports you will write. You must include your probable cause to stop, detain, and arrest the suspect. An arrest report also lays the groundwork for your probable cause to search for fruits or instrumentalities of the crime.

Clearance Reports

Clearance reports are used to document the disposition of a criminal case. Dispositions include arrest, identification of the suspect without arrest, recovery of property, restitution, or filing a criminal complaint. You seldom use clearance reports for noncriminal incidents.

Crime Reports

Crime reports, sometimes called "face-sheets," are completed when your preliminary investigation results in the conclusion that a crime occurred. The report documents your preliminary investigation and must include the *corpus delicti* or elements of the crime. It may also include suspect descriptions, property taken, evidence collected, property damage, and injuries to the victim. It should also include information about the suspect's modus operandi.

Daily Activity Reports

You may record your daily activity on a Daily Activity Report or Officer's Log. Typically, the report includes the location of the activity, amount of time spent, the names of people you talked to, and a brief disposition. In many agencies, you may use a mobile data terminal or laptop computer to record this information.

Evidence Reports

The collection and preservation of evidence at a crime scene may be documented in an evidence report. You use it to document the chain of evidence. You may also use it to request forensic examination of the evidence.

Incident Reports

Incident reports document events that are not crimes. Depending on the activity in your jurisdiction, 70 percent of your calls for service may not be crimes, for example, medical aid calls and civil disputes. In many of these cases, you will have to write a report documenting your actions. Incident reports may also be called service or miscellaneous reports.

Memorandums

A memo is a report written on a departmental form and is used to clarify the daily operation of the department. You may use memos to request information and to respond to requests for information. You frequently write memos concerning personnel requests, maintenance requests, and training.

Narcotics or Intoxication Reports

Narcotics or intoxication reports are used to document the suspect's condition when under the influence of drugs or alcohol. In opiate influence cases, the report may include a diagram showing the location of puncture wounds. It is not uncommon to complete an intoxication report for a suspect arrested for driving under the influence of alcohol and/or drugs or for public intoxication.

Supplemental Reports

In many cases, you are not the first officer on scene, yet you may still conduct part of the investigation. You will need to document your actions in a supplemental or follow-up report. You may also use a supplemental report to record information you discover after you have written the original report.

Traffic Accident Reports

Accident reports document the facts at the scene of a traffic collision. Your report may include statements of witnesses, diagrams, and photographs. Depending on your department's policy and state law, traffic officers may use a "short" form of the report for noninjury accidents.

USES AND PURPOSES OF REPORTS

Police reports are written at the scene of many events and, as a result, are used for a wide variety of reasons. You should remember that every report you write might be the one that "goes around the world" and is read by everyone.

Criminal Investigations

When you write a report documenting a criminal act, that report becomes the basis for coordination of the complete investigation and prosecution of the crime. It is also used to gain information for statistical reporting and crime analysis. Whether the investigation is conducted by patrol officers, general investigators, or a specialty unit of investigators, the original crime report is the source document. Initial crime reports are also used to compare past and current crimes to determine modus operandi and identify suspects.

Newspapers and the Media

Crime reports, and in some cases all reports, are available to the press and media. In most states, some parts of the crime reports may be deleted, for example, names of juvenile suspects and victims and the victims of certain crimes. However, in general, the press has the right of access to reports. The result is they read exactly what you have written, including misspellings and grammatical errors.

Reference Materials

Because reports are permanent documents, they provide an excellent source of historical information. They may be used to document the agency's actions, refresh your memory, or determine liability.

Statistical Data for Crime Analysis

The rapid development of computer technology, including expert systems and automated pin maps, has resulted in improved crime analysis. The source document for that information remains the crime report you write in the field. Your reports are used to identify trends, locations, and methods of operations. The result of that analysis may be directed patrol.

Documentation

Reports are used to document the action of the department and its officers. Because police departments are typically reactive, reports document what actions were taken to stop the criminal activity or arrest the suspect. They provide evidence of the department's responsiveness to the community and its needs.

Officer Evaluations

It is common for supervisors to use reports to evaluate an officer's performance. An experienced supervisor can determine your ability to organize information, level of education, technical knowledge, intelligence, and pride in the job. A report discloses an officer's weaknesses, weaknesses the officer may not even realize he or she has.

Statistical Reporting

Crime reports are the source document for the collection of statistical data. Agencies report crime statistics to various state and federal agencies. Statistical reports may also be generated for budget purposes, city council briefings, and other special-interest groups.

Report Writing Audience

Your reports must be self-explanatory because numerous people make decisions based on the information in your reports. Depending on the nature of the event, any or all of the following may read your report:

> *Police departments:* Supervisors and administrators of both your department and those cooperating in investigations
> *Attorneys:* Prosecution, defense, civil, and judges—all attorneys who may read your reports
> *Jurors:* In both criminal and civil trials
> *Administrators:* From your department and jurisdiction, as well as from city, county, and state jurisdictions
> *Medical professionals:* Doctors, psychiatrists, and psychologists
> *Corrections:* County jail and state and federal prison staff, including probation officers and parole agents
> *Insurance companies:* The parties involved in claims
> *Media:* Newspapers, radio, and television
> *Regulatory agencies:* Motor vehicle departments, insurance commissioners, alcohol beverage control, consumer affairs

If any part of your report requires further explanation, you have failed to accomplish your objectives. When you have to write a supplemental report to explain your original report, you create an air of skepticism. Your credibility may become questionable in the eyes of the court. You must not evade the necessity of well-written reports. It is important that you understand the merits of effective report writing and recognize the significance of reports in the total criminal justice system.

QUALITIES OF A GOOD REPORT

All police reports must contain certain qualities, which can be categorized as *accurate, clear, complete, concise, factual, objective,* and *prompt.*

and hearsay as though they were facts. Opinions, inferences, and suppositions are frequently based on logical premises; however, they can be based on prejudice and bias, thereby leaving you open for criticism.

Objective

You must remember there are always two sides to every story, and both sides have a right to be told. You must not be influenced by emotion, personal prejudice, or opinion. You collect and report the facts in an objective and professional manner.

Prompt

While you may not relish report writing, it is the most important task you will be routinely assigned. Your reports must be completed in a timely manner. If you arrest and book a suspect in jail, the suspect or his or her attorney is entitled to see the report as soon as possible. In some jurisdictions, judges or judicial hearing officers may review your report at the county jail to determine if there is probable cause for the arrest. Your reports must be completed as soon as possible. Your credibility may be open to speculation if this rule is not followed.

Learning Tip

Diagrams and photocopies make your reports more effective. Diagrams can convey facts even more accurately and briefly than a narrative explanation. Photocopies of some items, such as Miranda cards, consent search cards, and written notes or statements, may be attached to your reports. Other items, such as weapons, tools, or contraband, could also be copied and attached to reports. A copy of a three-dimensional object is worth a page of narrative and affects the reader more.

CHAPTER REVIEW

In this chapter, you learned what the definition of a report is and that there are ten different types of police reports. You also learned about the uses and purposes of police reports, how they are used, who uses them, and what makes a good report.

DISCUSSION QUESTIONS

1. What are the ten types of reports?
2. What are seven uses and purposes of reports?
3. Who makes up the report writer's audience?
4. What are the seven qualities of a good report?

EXERCISES

1. What type of report is used to document the events that occur when you arrest a suspect?
   a. Crime Report
   b. Incident Report
   c. Arrest Report
   d. Daily Activity Report

2. What type of report is used to document events that are not crimes?
   a. Crime Report
   b. Incident Report
   c. Arrest Report
   d. Daily Activity Report

3. What type of report is sometimes referred to as a "face-sheet"?
   a. Crime Report
   b. Incident Report
   c. Arrest Report
   d. Daily Activity Report

4. You are dispatched on a call to meet a resident at their home. When you arrive they tell you they just don't like their neighbor. The neighbor just moved in and hasn't said or done anything, the reporting party just doesn't like them. What type of report are you likely to write?
   a. Crime Report
   b. Incident Report
   c. Arrest Report
   d. Daily Activity Report

5. Why is it important for you to remember there are always two sides to every story when you're interviewing people? Because reports need to be:
   a. Prompt
   b. Concise
   c. Lengthy
   d. Objective

7

Report Writing Techniques

INTRODUCTION

The previous chapters provided you with English composition skills and general knowledge about the types of police reports. In this chapter, you will learn to apply your skills and knowledge to write police reports. Police report writing is considered technical writing, and as such you will need to develop special skills and techniques. Police report writing is the backbone of criminal investigations and prosecutions.

OBJECTIVES

At the end of this chapter, you will be able to do the following:

1. Define and explain interpersonal communications.
2. Identify the five steps of the report writing process.
3. Define chronological order.
4. Identify and write active-voice sentences.
5. Identify appropriate word usage for police reports.
6. Identify the advantages of first versus third person.
7. Properly use a tape recorder for note taking and report dictation.

"Just the facts Ma'am, please."

Your job in an interview is to listen to what people have to say.

INTERPERSONAL COMMUNICATION

You must understand the interpersonal communication process before you learn to conduct interviews and interrogations. One of your most valuable tools as a police officer is your interpersonal communication skill.

Definition of Communication

Generally, communication is defined as the use of language, spoken or written, to transfer information or exchange ideas. The transfer of information or ideas from one person to another includes the transmission and receipt of a message to effect some type of action or change.

Reasons for Communication

There are four reasons you communicate with other people:

1. *To provide adequate information for group living:* Police services are delivered to multicultural communities that include a growing elderly population. Your role as a police officer is rapidly changing from the traditional enforcer of laws to that of a service provider.

2. *To clarify perceptions and expectations:* The exchange of ideas and information is essential to clarify your perceptions and expectations and those of the community you serve.

3. *To stimulate creative thinking through feedback:* The human mind requires stimulation. You receive that stimulation from the feedback you receive during the communication process.

4. *To maintain your balance in the world:* During the communication process, you receive reinforcement or reassurance that you are okay.

Communication Process

The communication process contains a *sender,* a *receiver,* and the *feedback loop.* There is a continuous line of communication between the *sender* and *receiver.* They are linked together by the *feedback loop.* When you begin an interview, you are the *sender* because you ask questions. The person you are interviewing is the *receiver.* Both of you listen to and watch each other, which provides you *feedback.* When the person you're interviewing answers, your roles in the communication process change. Feedback includes the answers to questions, gestures, and expressions.

Types of Communication

You use nonverbal and verbal communication when dealing with people. Remember that you not only give off communication clues, but you should also practice reading the clues others give you.

Nonverbal Communication. You use three types of nonverbal communication: gestures, facial expressions, and body language.

Your gestures should be nonthreatening, using an open hand, for example. Facial expressions reveal your true feelings, so master appropriate expressions for every situation. Body language is easily read by others and conveys both your feelings and meanings. Positive use of body language will encourage people to talk and will improve your ability to gather information.

Verbal Communication. You may not realize it, but there are many different types of verbal communication; it is important for you to recognize and understand each type:

One-way communication is lecture or direction. It is effective in limited situations, especially where compliance without feedback is necessary. An example would be felony or high-risk car stops.

Two-way communication includes speaking and listening. You typically exchange information or ideas in two-way communication.

Oral-in-person communication means you can see and hear the person you are speaking to. You have the opportunity to use both verbal and nonverbal communication skills.

Oral-telephone communication is just what it sounds like, talking on the phone. The disadvantage is nonverbal communication is eliminated.

Written communication is the most difficult to master. You always disclose something about yourself in your writing. Typically, you disclose your ability to organize information, your educational level, and your technical expertise.

PRACTICE

Team up with another student in the class and alternate while doing the following:

Look at your partner and use your eyes and facial expressions to convey warmth and caring.

Look at your partner and use gestures to convey that "you mean business."

Look at your partner, smile, and say, "I'm going to fire you."

Look at your partner, smile, and say, "I'm always here to help you."

REPORT WRITING PROCESS

Police report writing is a five-step process. The steps are (1) interviewing, (2) note taking, (3) organizing and planning, (4) writing the narrative, and (5) proofreading. Your preliminary investigation includes report writing. During the investigation, you must complete each of the steps, or your final report will not be acceptable.

Interviewing

Interviewing is the first step in the process. Your interviews of victims, witnesses, and suspects are the backbone of your preliminary investigation. Frequently, the first officer at the scene of a crime has the best opportunity to solve the crime by conducting a thorough preliminary investigation. If you do not conduct successful interviews, your preliminary investigation and police report will not be acceptable.

Three-Step Interview Method.   The three-step interview method is an easy way for you to conduct interviews. It is structured to allow your informant to speak at ease while you have control over the interview. While you are learning, practice on simple interview situations. After you feel comfortable, you will be able to use this three-step method for interviews and interrogations:

1. *Subject tells the story:* You listen, keeping the subject on track and giving verbal and nonverbal clues to keep the story flowing.

You don't attempt to take notes during this first step. During this step, you accomplish the following:

Establish rapport with the subject.
Determine what crime, if any, occurred.
Determine what agency has jurisdiction.
Detect signs of untruthfulness or discrepancies.
Determine what action you should take.

2. *Subject retells the story and you take notes:* You gather identifying information about the subject and ask questions about the incident as you guide the subject through the story a second time. During this step, you accomplish the following:

Determine the chronological order of the events.
Establish the *corpus delicti* of the crime.
Ask questions in the order you want to write the report (thereby organizing your report as you take notes).

3. *You read your notes to the subject:* When you do this, you are actually writing your report for the first time. What you are reading is going to be what you write in your report. During this step, the subject can correct errors or remember additional information, and you can correct errors or ask additional questions.

Learning Tip

Use of the three-step interview method adds credibility to your courtroom testimony. You can testify that you always use the same method, following the same three steps, in all the interviews you conduct. If there is a discrepancy between the informant's courtroom testimony and what you've written in your report, your use of the three-step method documents your actions.

Interrogation. In general, there is one difference between an interview of a subject and the interrogation of a suspect: *focus.* An interrogation is a planned interview with the primary focus being to obtain a confession or eliminate the person as a suspect. A secondary focus may be to find incriminating evidence. Generally, when you interview a victim or witness, you are not sure what he or she is going to tell you. When you interrogate a suspect, you have probably already collected substantial information about the incident and have a pretty good idea what the suspect is going to say. During most interrogations, police officers don't ask questions they don't know the answers to. That doesn't mean you will get the answer you anticipated.

You use the same interpersonal communication skills in both situations. That's why it is important for you to develop the ability to use both your verbal and nonverbal skills. In some cases, you may have several questions written down to ask a suspect during the interrogation. There is nothing in an interrogation to justify coercion, excessive force, or violation of a suspect's constitutional rights. Because case law changes rapidly and may vary from state to state, you should review legal updates and department training bulletins regularly.

Note Taking

Notes are defined as brief notations concerning specific events that are recorded while they are fresh in your mind and used to prepare a report.

Types of Notes. There are two types of notes: *permanent* and *temporary*. If you use permanent notes, you must keep those notes in a safe storage place. If you elect to use temporary notes, you must discard your notes after completing your report. Whichever type of notes you elect to use, you must not change back and forth based on the type of report. If you do change the type of notes you take from call to call, defense attorneys may attack your credibility by asking why you keep some notes and discard others.

It is recommended you use permanent notes. Recording your notes on a note pad or steno pad provides you with a reference and resource book. You will always have access to your original source of information.

Purposes of Notes. Notes are the basis for your report. You take notes to assist your memory with specific details, such as names, dates of birth, serial numbers, addresses, and phone numbers. If you take neat and accurate notes and they are subpoenaed into court, they add to your credibility and demonstrate your high level of proficiency and professionalism. A good defense attorney may attempt to develop impeachable inconsistencies between your notes and your report.

Scratch Outline. You should use a *scratch* or informal outline for taking notes. Scratch outlines provide a simple, structured, easy way to organize the information on your note pad during step 2 of the three-step interview method.

A scratch outline has a key sentence followed by supporting points. The supporting points are written under the key sentence and indented from the left margin. Neither the key sentence nor supporting points are numbered or lettered.

Example:

Key sentence	Ofc. Cleveland arrested Rusty Hodges for burglary
Supporting points	victim saw Hodges
	Hodges ran from Ofc. Cleveland
	Cleveland caught Hodges
	Hodges had the victim's license

Scratch outlines don't have a set format. Use your own style and develop something useful for you.

The questions you ask in step 2 of the interview are generally your key sentences. The informant's responses are your supporting points. Don't try to write down everything the subject tells you, unless you're going to quote him. Remember, notes are *brief notations,* just enough to remind you at a later time when you are writing your report.

Scratch outlining may sound familiar to you. Teachers use a similar method to teach writing and paragraphing. A key sentence is the same as a topic sentence. The difference between police report writing and English composition is the source of information and the method used to collect it. Most of the information in a police report comes from interviews you conduct.

When you are taking notes, remember to leave spaces between the lines and don't try to use every inch of the page. You may need to add additional information or correct something you have already written down. You will also need space when you begin to organize your report.

Organizing and Planning

The organizing and planning of your report is the third step. If your report is properly organized and planned, it will be clear, easy to read, understandable, and concise. The small amount of time you spend on organizing and planning greatly reduces the time you spend rewriting reports.

Organizing and planning your report begins during the three-step interview method. During step 2, ask questions in the order that you want to include the information in your narrative. Organizing and planning your narrative is closely related to chronological order, which is discussed later in this chapter. Ask questions in the order the event took place, which is the chronological order of the event, and it will make writing your narrative much easier.

Once the informant has told you his or her story during step 1 of the three-step interview, you can begin organizing and planning your report. You will know the chronological order of the event, so ask questions in that order during step 2 of the interview.

Review your scratch outline and verify the information you will need to include in the narrative. You may want to underline, number, or otherwise mark important points in your notes. In some cases, you may even draw arrows to remind you where to include information in the narrative. You should also consider the information you want to omit from the narrative.

Writing the Narrative

You may not believe it, but writing the narrative should be the easiest part of report writing. If you have carefully followed the three-step interview method (properly taken notes) and spent a few minutes organizing and planning, writing the narrative is almost anticlimactic. If you use the methods described above, you will be prepared to write reports using the one-write system, dictation, or a laptop computer.

Just before you begin to write the narrative, stop and think about what you have done and what you have left to do. You have collected all the appropriate information, determined your actions, taken notes, and actually recited the report out loud during step 3 of the interview. Your notes, in scratch outline format, are the road map for writing the narrative. The key sentences generally remind you to start a new paragraph, and the supporting points are used to write the sentences. If you practice following these steps, you will find writing the narrative really is the easiest part.

Proofreading

You may think writing the narrative is the final step, but it's not. When you have finished writing the narrative, proofread it. Most officers are just thankful to have finished the report and don't take the additional moment or two to review their work. Think about who else is going to read the report. Depending on the type of report and whether or not you've arrested a suspect, your report will be read by sergeants, investigators, prosecutors, defense attorneys, and judges. If you have made an arrest, the defense attorney's best chance to defend his or her client comes from your report.

Check for the following when you proofread:

Correct report form(s) and format
Probable cause to stop, detain, arrest, search, and seize
Corpus delicti, the elements of the offense
Correct spelling
Active-voice sentence structure
Proper punctuation

The last things to ask yourself when proofreading are as follows: Is this report the best I can do? Would I want to read it to the chief of police or to a jury? Is there anything else I can do to make it better?

PRACTICE

Team up with another student in the class and choose one of the following questions to interview each other, using the three-step interview method and scratch outlining for note taking:

Tell me everything you've done today, from the time you woke up.

Tell me about your last job.

CHRONOLOGICAL ORDER

You must understand chronological order to write coherent and accurate police reports. Your reports should not skip around or jump from topic to topic. Frequently, officers' reports will jump from interview to interview, which makes the report confusing and difficult to follow. If you use the three-step interview method and scratch outlining, you shouldn't have any trouble with chronological order.

Definition

For the purposes of police report writing, chronological order is defined as the arrangement of events and/or actions in order by the time of their occurrence. Simply stated: in order, what happened and when.

There are usually two chronological orders to an event: the order of the officer's activities and the order of the event. The exception is when you initiate the activity (for example, an observation arrest), and you become a participant in the event.

Generally, you first interview the victim, then the witness, then the suspect, and finally tell your sergeant what happen.

Officer's Order of Activity

The order of your activities should be the easiest for you to follow. You will have not only your memory but also your notes. It is recommended that you write your reports in the order of your activity. This style is frequently called narrative report writing. (Category style is discussed later in this chapter.)

Think of a residential burglary where the victim calls the police and wants to make a report. What do you do after you receive the radio call?

Interview the victim.
Search for and interview any witnesses.
Search for and possibly arrest the suspect.
Account for your activities.

You would write the narrative in the above example in that same order. First, write about the victim interview, then your search for witnesses, their interview(s), your search for the suspect(s), and so on.

Order of the Event

The order of the event is the arrangement of occurrences and/or actions as they occurred during the crime. When did the suspect enter the house, what did he take, when did he leave, what was he driving, and what was his direction of travel? Every witness may have a different version of the chronological order of the event because they may not have seen the same things.

Using the above example, the following scratch outline demonstrates the chronological order of an event as you might write it in your notes.

Example:

Victim:	left at 7 P.M. to go to the movies
	returned at 10:30 P.M.
	front door was open
	VCR and camcorder were missing from family room
	called police
Witness:	lives next door at 9380
	8:00 P.M. saw suspect walk across victim's yard
	carry camcorder to car
	white Chevrolet, license ABC 123
You:	11:00 P.M. saw suspect car on Main St.
	verified license number
	stopped and arrested suspect
	saw VCR and camcorder on seat
	Mirandized suspect and interviewed
Suspect:	went to house at 8:00 P.M.
	no one answered doorbell

	twisted knob with vise grips
	took VCR and camcorder
You:	booked suspect at county jail
	returned property to victim

Officer-Initiated Activity (Observation)

When you make an observation arrest or see an event take place, you become an active participant and there is only one chronological order. A good example would be if you saw someone smoking marijuana. Your observations and actions are part of the report. You document your actions and those of someone else.

Example:

You:	see suspect sitting on a park bench
	smoking a marijuana cigarette
	confiscate the dope
	interview the suspect
Suspect:	admits it is his dope
You:	arrest suspect
	book the evidence

Spatial Order

Spatial order defines the position of objects within a given environment. At a crime scene, it means the location of all physical evidence and objects. The spatial order you should be aware of is the location of items of evidence in relationship to each other. When you describe the crime scene, you would move logically from left to right, top to bottom, and so forth. You always want to describe what you see in a logical order, not jump from one object or location to another, so the reader has a clear picture of the crime scene.

Example:

I approached the open bedroom door, looked inside, and saw the following: The light switch was on the left wall, and the switch was on. To the left of the light switch, I saw a hole in the wall. I saw a bed along the same wall under the hole. There wasn't anything else in the room. The light on the ceiling was broken. I saw a blood-stained area on the carpet beneath the ceiling light.

Category Style

You may work for an agency that prefers officers write in category style. Category style requires you to use specific subheadings in the specific order dictated by your department's report writing manual.

Example:

Source: I received a radio call about a subject in the park smoking marijuana.

Officer's observations: I arrived at 1345 hours and saw Jones sitting on a park bench. He was smoking what appeared to be a marijuana cigarette.

Suspect statements: Jones said it was his marijuana.

While category style can be cumbersome and inconvenient, it does provide a guide or checklist for you to follow.

PRACTICE

The following facts are pertinent to a theft report. Read each statement and decide the correct chronological order for your report. Place 1 by the first fact, 2 by the second, and so on until all statements have been put in order:

_____ The red and white bicycle was worth $100.

_____ The movie was over about 2:15 and she rode straight home.

_____ She came out of the house about thirty minutes later.

_____ No one had permission to take the bicycle.

_____ She left it parked on the front porch.

_____ The bicycle was gone.

ACTIVE-VOICE WRITING STYLE

You learned in Chapter Six that police reports should be clear and concise. Clear means plain or evident to the mind of the reader. Concise means your report says as much as possible in as few words as possible. The best way to have both of these qualities in your reports is to write in active voice. If you use active voice, your reports will be easier to read.

The alternative to active voice is passive voice. Passive-voice sentences are weak and confusing and may not identify the doer of the action.

Active-voice writing style allows you to:

Reduce sentence length by 20 percent.
Directly answer the question, Who did the action?
Eliminate punctuation errors.
Avoid weak and awkward sentences.

Examples:
I wrote the citation. (active voice)
The citation was written by me. (passive voice)

THREE STEPS TO DETERMINE ACTIVE VOICE

Use the following three steps to write in the active voice:

1. Locate the *action* (verb) of the sentence.
2. Locate who or what is doing the action. This is the *doer* (subject) of the sentence. If the *doer* is implied and not written in or is being acted on by the *action*, the sentence is weak or passive. If the *doer* is written but not located just in front of the *action*, the sentence is weak.
3. Put the *doer* immediately in front of the *action*.

Examples:
The officer wrote the citation. (active voice)
The dispatcher repeated the address. (active voice)
A suspect was arrested. (passive voice)

Using the above steps, correct the last statement:

1. What is the *action* of the sentence? *was arrested*
2. Who or what is the *doer* of the action? The sentence doesn't have a *doer*, so who made the arrest? *I*
3. Put the *doer* immediately in front of the *action*: I arrested the suspect.

PRACTICE

Determine if these sentences are active or passive voice; use an A for active and a P for passive:

_____ The sergeant read the crime warning.

_____ The suspect didn't resist arrest.

_____ The meeting was called by the chief.

_____ It was determined by the victim what was missing.

_____ Several citations were written by the motor officer.

OBJECTIVE REPORT WRITING

You learned the importance of objective reports in Chapter Six. While you may write only factual statements in your reports, it is possible they are not objective. In your police reports, objective means you weren't influenced by emotion or prejudice. Your writings are fair, impartial, and not opinionated.

Your reports can lose objectivity because of poor word usage, omission of facts, and uncontrolled personal feelings. You maintain your objectivity by using nonemotional words, including both sides of every story, and remaining a professional during all investigations.

Nonemotional Words

You should use *denotative* words, words that are explicit and non-emotional. Emotional words are called *connotative* because they suggest or imply something beyond the explicit or literal meaning of the word.

> **Examples:**
> bureaucrat, blubbered, scream, wail (connotative)
> public employee, civil servant, cried, wept, yell (denotative)

Slanting

You slant your report when you fail to include both sides of the event. You must include statements from all the witnesses, victims, suspects, or participants. When you omit all or part of someone's statement, no matter how unusual, you have slanted your report and lost objectivity.

PRACTICE

Circle the denotative word in each example:

> woman/broad, officer/cop, confused/crazy,
> uncooperative/hostile, argue/verbal confrontation

WORD USAGE

Police officers from all regions of the country tend to use similar words and phrases. Unfortunately, these words and phrases are not necessarily the best choices for clarity, objectivity, and conciseness. In most cases, officers don't use them in everyday conversation. While you shouldn't write the way you talk, you should try to use everyday words that everyone will understand.

Deadwood Words

These words and phrases are fancy, formal, or grand expressions that usually serve no purpose. You should use common, everyday words that are understood by everyone, especially judges and jurors.

Instead Of	*Try*
abeyance	delayed or held up
accomplish, execute, perform	do
accordingly	therefore, so, that is why
accumulate	gather
acquaint	tell
acquire, secure	get
additional	added

"The cereal killer stood over the corps holding the steal pipe in his write hand..."

Make sure the words in your report are what you meant to say.

Instead Of	*Try*
ad infinitum	endlessly
adverse	poor, bad
advise	write, inform, tell
afford an opportunity	allow, permit, let
aforementioned, aforesaid	these
aggregate	total
a good deal	much
a great deal of the time	often
a limited quantity of	few
all of	all
along the lines	like, the same way
alteration, revision	change
altercation	fight
ameliorate	improve
analyzation	analysis
answer in the affirmative	say yes
anticipate	foresee
apparent	clear

Instead Of	*Try*
appears that	is clear
appended	added
applicable	apply to
are desirous of	want
are in receipt of	have received
as a matter of fact	in fact
ascertain	discover, find out
as per	according to
assistance	aid, help
assuming that	if
at a later date	later
at an early date	soon
at such time	when
attached you will find	attached is
at the present time	now
attribute to	due to
balance	remainder, rest
basis, based on, on the basis of	on, by, after, for, because
be in position to	can
beneficial aspects of	benefits
broken down into	divided into
bulk of	most
by means of	by, with
check into	check
classifications	classes
close proximity	near, close
cognizance	knowledge
cognizant of	know
commence	start
commitment	promise
compensate, compensation	pay, payment
concur	agree
consensus of opinion	consensus
consequently	so
considerable	much, serious, grave
consider favorably	approve
construct	build
contacted	spoke to, visited
contingent upon receipt of	when we receive
continuous basis	continually
contribute	give
deleterious, detrimental	harmful
demonstrate	show
despite the fact that	although
direct effort toward	try
due in large measure to	due largely to
due to the fact that	because
during the course of	during
during the time that	while

Instead Of	*Try*
effect a reduction of	reduce
employ	use
encounter	meet
endeavor	try
equivalent	equal
excessive amount	too much
exit	leave
expedite	hasten, hurry, speed
expense	cost
explicit	plain
facilitate	make easy, simplify
feasible	possible
feels	believes, thinks
finalize	finish, end
following	after
forthcoming	coming
for the purpose of	for, to
for the reason that	because, since
found to be	are
forward, furnish, transmit	send
frequently	often
furthermore	also, in addition
gainfully employed	working, employed
give consideration to	consider
give instruction to	instruct, teach
have a need for	need
henceforth, hereafter	from now on, in the future
herein	here
hereinafter	after this
hereinbefore	until now
heretofore	up to now, until now
herewith	with this, now
imminent	near (in time)
implement	carry out, set up, enforce
in accordance with	with, by, as, under
in advance of, prior to	before
in a most careful manner	carefully
in a number of cases	some, many
inasmuch as	because
in a timely manner	promptly
in connection with	with
indebtedness	debt
indicate, state	show, tell, say, note
initial	first
initiate	begin, start
in large measure	largely
in lieu of	instead of
in many cases	many

Instead Of	*Try*
in order that	so
in order to	to
in regard to	concerning
in relation to	about
in spite of the fact that	although
institute	start, begin
in the affirmative	yes, agreed
in the amount of	for
in the course/case of	in, at, or, during, while
in the event of/that	if
in the magnitude of	about
in the majority of cases	usually
in the matter of	in, about
in the time of	during
in the very near future	soon
in the vicinity of	near
in this day and age	today
in view of the fact	since, because
is as follows	follows
it is my understanding that	I understand
it is our opinion	we feel, we believe
it should be noted that	furthermore
justification for	reason for
kindly arrange to send	please send
locality	place
locate	find, put
likewise	and also
maintenance	upkeep
make a decision	decide
make a determination	determine
make application for	apply
make inquiry regarding	ask
modification	change
negative results	found nothing
nevertheless	but, however
nonavailability of	unavailable
notwithstanding	despite, in spite of
numerous	many
objective	aim
obligate	bind
obligation	debt
observed	saw
obtain	get
occasion	cause
on a few occasions	occasionally
on behalf of	for
on the basis of	by, from, because
on the grounds that	because
on the occasion of	when

Instead Of	*Try*
on the part of	for, among
on the subject of	about
optimum	the most for the least
orientated	oriented
outside of	outside
owing to the fact that	because
participate	take part
per diem, per annum	per day, per year
pertain	about, on
peruse	read
place emphasis on	emphasize
possess	have
preventative	preventive
prior to	before
proceed	go
procure	get
provided, providing	if
realize a savings of	save
regarding	about
reimburse	pay
related with, relates to, relating to, relative to	on, about
render aid or assistance	help
reported	said, told
resided	lived
residence	house, apartment
responded	answered, said
sibling	brother, sister
subject matter	subject, topic
submit	send, give
subsequently, subsequent to	later, afterward, then, next
sufficient	enough
summarization	summary
sustained	received
take action	act
terminate, terminated	end, stop, ended, stopped
the question as to whether	whether
thereafter	after that, then
the reason is due to	because
therein	there, in it
thereof	of it
thereupon	then
this is a subject that	this subject
transmit	send
transported	took, drove
under date of	on
under the circumstances	because
until such time as	until

Instead Of	*Try*
utilization, utilize	use
vehicle	car, truck
visualize	see, think of, imagine
whereby	by which, so that
wherein	in which, where, when
whether or not	whether
wish to advise, wish to state	(avoid, do not use)
without further delay	immediately, soon, quickly
with regard to,	about, regarding,
with reference to,	concerning
with respect to	
with the result that	so that
would seem, would appear	seem/appear (try to
	avoid these)

Slang

Slang is usually a coinage or nonstandard vocabulary developed by a group of people. You may be familiar with street slang, drug slang, and police slang. It is inappropriate to use slang in your report, unless you are quoting someone.

Examples:

ran/split, arrested/busted, in possession/holding, under the influence/down

Jargon

Jargon is usually the specialized language of a profession. Criminal justice professionals, just like other professionals, use a great deal of jargon. You should not use jargon in your reports.

Examples:

undefined penal codes; 187 PC
radio codes; 503, 1199
drunk driver; deuce

Word Meanings

You should always make sure you know the correct definition and spelling of the words you use in your reports. The following words are frequently misused because of a lack of understanding of correct meaning, definition, or usage:

Already: by this or a specified time
All ready: all things are ready
Among: three or more in a group
Between: in a position between two or an interval separating
Appear to: to come into view, become visible

Seem to: to give the impression of being
As: to the same extent or degree, equally
When: at what time
Canvas: a heavy, coarse fabric
Canvass: to examine thoroughly or to solicit
Counsel: consultation or a lawyer
Council: a body of people elected by voters
Effect (noun): a result, the way something acts on an object
Affect (verb): to have an influence on, impress
Elude: to evade or escape
Allude: to make an indirect reference to
Past: no longer current
Passed: moved on ahead, proceeded
Principle: a basic truth, a law
Principal: foremost in rank or worth, a person
Stationary: not moving, not capable of being moved
Stationery: writing paper
Trustee: a person or agent in a position of trust
Trusty: an inmate worker in prison or jail
Upon: on, to put on top of
When: at what time

Euphemisms

A euphemism is a polite or diplomatic way to say something that might otherwise be taken as an insult or uncomplimentary remark. You should be specific and professional in your reports and avoid using euphemisms. Euphemisms can mislead the reader.

Officers frequently are embarrassed or self-conscious when investigating sex crimes or child abuse cases, and they will use euphemisms for anatomical parts of the body. You should use the correct terms.

Examples:
penis/private parts, bra and panties/unmentionables,
used/previously owned car, obese/weight problem,
argue/verbal confrontation, refused to answer/uncooperative

FIRST PERSON AND THIRD PERSON

You may write your reports in either the first- or third-person style. Both are acceptable; however, first-person style is preferred and the most widely used. You should refer to yourself as an active participant. Third-person writing style for police reports is archaic and outdated. "I" isn't poison.

The alternative to first person is third person. You refer to yourself as assigned officer, reporting officer, or this officer.

Usually, department policy specifies which style you use. If given the choice, use first person. Police reports should be written in an easily understandable style. When you interview a victim, witness, or suspect, you are actively involved.

Examples:

I talked to Mrs. Smith. (first person)

Officer Jones and I searched the building. (first person)

This officer talked to Mrs. Smith. (third person)

Assigned officer and his partner searched the building. (third person)

PARAGRAPHS

You may want to review the section on note taking and the use of the scratch outline. Scratch outlines have key sentences, and those key sentences are generally topic sentences in paragraphing. If you take good notes during the interview process, you should have no trouble understanding paragraphing.

A paragraph is a group of sentences that tells about one topic. The topic sentence tells what the sentences in the paragraph are about. Usually, it is the first sentence in the paragraph. Paragraphing is a method of alerting the reader to a shift in focus in the report.

Steps in Writing a Paragraph

First, your notes provide the key or topic sentence and the outline for the paragraphs. Check for completeness and rearrange sentences if necessary.

Second, write the paragraph in active-voice style, using 12- to 15-word sentences. Paragraphs in police reports generally have five to seven sentences or approximately 100 words. However, it is acceptable in police reports to write one- or two-sentence paragraphs. One- or two-sentence paragraphs are used to mark a transition in reports from one topic or section to another (typically, going from the interview of the victim to the interview of a witness). Indent the beginning of each paragraph or skip one or two lines between paragraphs.

Third, proofread your work. If necessary, correct mistakes and rewrite the paragraph or report.

When writing a paragraph, keep the following factors in mind.

Unity.   Preserve the unity of the paragraph. A paragraph should develop a single topic, the key sentence. Every sentence in the paragraph should contribute to the development of that single idea.

Coherence.   Compose the paragraph so it reads coherently. Coherence makes it easy for the reader to follow the facts and events. It reflects clear thinking by the report writer. A clearly stated chronological order of events makes the paragraph and therefore the report coherent.

Development.   Paragraphs should be adequately developed. The first step is to consider the central idea. Present examples or specific quotes. Include relevant facts, details, or evidence. Explore and explain the causes of an event or the motives of the suspect. The result may be an explanation of how the event occurred. Finally, describe the scene, injuries, or other pertinent information.
Consider the following suggestions:

Repeat key sentences from paragraph to paragraph.

Use pronouns in place of key nouns.

Use "pointing words," for example, *this, that, these,* and *those*.

Use "thought-connecting words," such as *however, moreover, also, nevertheless, therefore, thus, subsequently, indeed, then,* and *accordingly*.

Arrange sentences in chronological order.

USE OF TAPE RECORDERS

You may consider using a tape recorder for both note taking and report dictation.

Note Taking

The use of a tape recorder for field note taking is generally discouraged. The biggest problem with tape recording field notes is that you capture too much unnecessary information. You may elect to use a tape recorder for note taking if you are interviewing a suspect in an involved or serious crime.

If you use a tape recorder for interviews, at the beginning of the interview, always include the following:

Your name, rank, and department

Date and time

Case number and type of case

Tape recorders may play an important role in obtaining suspects' unsolicited statements where there is no violation of their constitutional rights. Under current case law, a suspect has no reasonable expectation to privacy in a police car. Therefore, officers may place a tape recorder in a patrol car and record suspect conversations.

Remember, there is no substitute for good note taking.

Report Dictation

You will find that dictating reports is much easier if you follow the three-step interview and scratch outline note-taking methods. The combination of these two methods is called a *dictation tree*. Some agencies now use dictation systems that have limited word processing capabilities.

Eleven Dictation Tips

1. Organize your thoughts by reviewing your notes.
2. Relax for a few minutes after reviewing your notes.
3. State the type of report (what form to use) and your name and badge number when you first begin to dictate.
4. Follow the order of the blocks on the form.
5. Slow your speech slightly.
6. Speak clearly; spell out names and words that are not easily understood.
7. Do not lose concentration; don't try to listen for radio calls and the like.
8. Do not smoke, drink, chew gum, or eat during dictation.
9. Pause if you make a mistake; then tell the operator that you need to make a correction.
10. Restate your name and badge number when you are finished.
11. Use simple courtesy (for example, "Thank you, operator").

CHAPTER REVIEW

In this chapter, you learned to apply your skills and knowledge to write police reports. You can define and explain interpersonal communication, identify the five steps of the report writing process, define chronological order, identify and write active-voice sentences, identify appropriate word usage for police reports, identify the advantages of first versus third person, and properly use a tape recorder for note taking and report dictation.

DISCUSSION QUESTIONS

1. Explain why interpersonal communication skills are important to police officers.
2. Identify two of the four reasons we communicate, and discuss their importance and meaning.
3. Define and explain nonverbal communication.
4. What are the three steps in the three-step interview method, and what does each accomplish?
5. Explain the value of three-step interviewing and scratch outlining when writing paragraphs.

EXERCISES

Revise the following sentences so they are clear, concise, and jargon- and slang-free.

1. The subject exited the stolen vehicle post hastily.

   _____

2. A theft in amount of $34.83 was reported.

   _____

3. The officer detected the odor of burning marijuana.

   _____

4. Officers contacted Lewis at his home.

   _____

5. The detective named Robinson as their primary suspect on account of the fact that his fingerprints matched those detectives found at the crime scene.

   _____

   _____

Replace each of the following words or phrases with a simple word or phrase.

1. Adjacent to   _____

2. Altercation   _____

3. Transported   _____

4. Observed   _____

5. Ascertain   _____

Choose the correct word in each of the following sentences.

1. The (affect/effect) of the medication began to (affect/effect) his judgment.

2. The burglar parked the car in the (alley/ally).

3. The driver said he could not (brake/break) in time to avoid the accident.

4. As the mortally wounded victim was (dying/dyeing), he named his assailant.

5. The building was a strange (local/locale) for the gathering.

"Observed law violator,
arrested same."

Make sure your word choice results in a clear, concise police report. The language of your report must be simple and to the point.

6. Always use a (stationary/stationery) object when you need a point of reference.

7. The investigators made a (through/thorough) investigation.

8. Officers will (advice/advise) the suspects of their rights.

9. The forgery suspect tried to (altar/alter) his appearance.

10. The whole neighborhood could (breath/breathe) easier once the police caught the escaped murderer.

Determine if these sentences are active or passive voice. If they are passive, rewrite them in active voice.

1. All the money was given to the suspect by the teller.

_____

2. The suspect took the money and ran out the door.

_____

3. A radio broadcast of the suspect's description was put out by me.

_____

4. Two blocks away, the suspect was stopped by Officer Wright.

_____

5. The suspect was identified by the witness.

_____

Remember, your report accurately reflects what happened, even if you're in "hot-pursuit."

Student Workbook

CHAPTER ONE PARTS OF SPEECH

Identify the parts of speech in the following sentences.

1. The officers carefully patrolled the neighborhood after the shooting incident.

2. No one could easily identify the three suspects from the descriptions.

3. Officer Sanchez left the patrol car and searched the area on foot.

4. Mrs. Ngyun told the officers, "I would recognize the thief the minute I saw him again."

5. Mr. Irving said he was very cautious when he opened the door because he smelled smoke.

6. No patrol should be routine for any officer.

7. Witherspoon denied his guilt in the murder but admitted his hatred of the store owner.

8. The investigators will store the evidence for the upcoming trial in the evidence locker.

9. The crowd demanded justice but really wanted revenge.

10. Two of the suspects surrendered inside the building, but the third suspect had quietly sneaked behind some trash cans in the alley before Officer Brooker caught him.

CHAPTER TWO SENTENCE ELEMENTS

Complete Sentences

Label the following sentences as complete (C), fragment (F), or run-on (R). Correct all fragments and run-ons.

_____   1. Halt!

_____

_____

_____   2. The two officers left at 0300, what time is it now?

_____

_____

_____   3. Until the investigators were able to sift through the evidence and learn the truth.

_____

_____

_____   4. Mario was reluctant to testify because the gang members frightened him; yet, he knew his story could save the defendant's life.

_____

_____

_____   5. Although Riley practiced shooting and carefully cleaned his gun after practice on the pistol range, and made every effort to improve.

_____

_____

_____   6. Why he did it he didn't know, he knew he couldn't get away with it.

_____

_____

_____   7. Although dazed from the injuries she received in the accident, Ms. Demont was still able to help the occupants from the other car.

_____

_____

_____   8. The investigator asked the bystanders if anyone had seen anything but no one wanted to get involved they were afraid of retaliation.

_____

_____

——— 9. Train your mind to work efficiently and to catch minor mistakes.

_____

_____

——— 10. Remember to check your reports for sentence fragments and run-ons because an otherwise excellent police officer can appear less than competent if his or her reports contain these common writing errors.

_____

_____

Subjects and Verbs

Underline the simple subject once and the verb twice.

1. A picture of the suspect appeared in the paper.

2. The gang members scrubbed the wall, sanded it, and repainted it just to remove the graffiti.

3. There must have been fifteen witnesses to the bank robbery.

4. Write your notes clearly the first time.

5. Magazines, beer bottles, and partially smoked cigarettes were scattered around the room.

Circle the correct form of the verb in the following sentences.

1. Neither the suspect nor his accomplices (was/were) caught.

2. The mayor's use of statistics (make/makes) him sound important.

3. The van, but not its contents, (was/were) recovered.

4. The squad (has/have) chosen a new spokesperson.

5. Either the investigators or their captain (need/needs) to issue a statement.

Revise the following sentences.

1. There was only the suspect and the complainant in the room at the time.

_____

_____

2. Any one of those people were capable of committing the crime.

   _____

   _____

3. We need more traffic officers at Grand and Main; is any available?

   _____

   _____

4. Each of his fellow officers have contributed to the fund.

   _____

   _____

5. Among the suspects was a local pimp, a pusher, and an ex-con.

   _____

   _____

6. The report gave an account of the incident, and then the investigator asks more questions.

   _____

   _____

7. They commit the crime at 0440 hours and stole the car at 0500 hours.

   _____

   _____

8. The burglar quietly opens the door and then walked quickly down the hall.

   _____

   _____

9. The investigators kept trying to call the victim for weeks, but they didn't know he's already moved.

   _____

   _____

10. The hit-and-run driver went home and tells her husband what happened.

    _____

    _____

Irregular Verbs

In the space provided, write the correct past tense form of the verb.

1. The witness said she (see)_____the suspect enter the house.

2. He had (steal)_____things in the past.

3. The investigators have (do)_____all the investigation work and (write)_____all the reports.

4. He should have (bring)_____all the information with him.

5. He (drink)_____so much beer that he had too much to drive home.

6. Rookies sometimes find they have not (take)_____enough notes to write their narratives.

7. The captain had (give)_____the new officers instructions and (show)_____them what to do.

8. Officer Windom had already (eat)_____when she received the call.

9. The burglar was (go)_____before the sleepy residents (know)_____that anything had been (take)_____.

10. The body (lie)_____on the floor, but the coroner could not tell exactly how long it had (lie)_____there.

Direct Objects, Indirect Objects, and Subject Complements

Underline the direct objects and/or subject complements in the following sentences. Circle any indirect objects you find.

1. The forensic department studied the evidence carefully.

2. Witnesses showed the officers the evidence.

3. The report was the main focus of the attorney's objections.

4. Officer Kim read the suspect his rights.

5. Captain Foster was the only officer available.

6. The injured driver was lying beside the road.

7. The racketeer grew more powerful and greedy as his influence increased.

8. The hostages remained calm throughout the ordeal.

9. The city council gave the department a new contract with better benefits.

10. Which investigator did you want?

Modifiers

Underline the misplaced or dangling modifiers in the following sentences. Then correct the errors. In some cases, you will have to rewrite the sentences.

1. Officer Nova found six marijuana cigarettes outside the car rolled with toilet paper.

   _____

   _____

2. The traffic controller watched the nine-car crash that happened on their closed-circuit TV monitor.

   _____

   _____

3. Officer Lemon killed the dog that attacked her with a single shot.

   _____

   _____

4. The supervisor told her he needed someone who could type badly.

   _____

   _____

5. After years of being lost in a back room filing cabinet, Stanley P. Duefuss found all the old case records.

   _____

   _____

6. I saw that the police had captured the murderer in the evening paper.

   _____

   _____

7. Officer Clark confiscated the switchblade from the suspect with a carved ivory handle.

   _____

   _____

8. Officers saw a suspicious van parked behind the building with two occupants in it.

_____

_____

9. Once coated with plastic, no one could alter the new identification cards.

_____

_____

10. The attorney only questioned these witnesses.

_____

_____

CHAPTER THREE PRONOUNS

Circle the correct pronoun form from the choices in parentheses.

1. The watch commander asked each officer to list (his/their) duty preferences.

2. Investigators found everyone home except (he/him) and his father.

3. The lieutenant left the final decision up to (we/us) officers.

4. When an officer is always late to briefing, (you/they/he) should expect a reprimand.

5. (Officer Ramirez and he/Officer Ramirez and him) followed the suspect's car.

6. The new captain called Officer Ngyun and (I/me) into his office.

7. Everyone was giving the officer (their/his or her) opinion at the same time.

8. Each division needed to submit (its/it's) budget requests.

9. All of the expended rounds of ammunition (was/were) confiscated.

10. The customers (who/which) were injured received medical treatment.

Circle and correct the agreement problems in these sentences.

1. The officer caught the suspect, but he slashed him on the arm.

_____

_____

2. The witness said she saw someone near the door, but they didn't come in.

   _____

   _____

3. Several people saw the suspects get out of the car. They went into the old building.

   _____

   _____

4. If one wants to succeed, you must work hard.

   _____

   _____

5. One can work happily if you like what you're doing.

   _____

   _____

6. Anyone who violates the law should be aware of the risk they are taking.

   _____

   _____

7. Officer Clay told the victim that he could call his doctor if he didn't feel well.

   _____

   _____

8. That dog's owner should be jailed. He howls all night.

   _____

   _____

9. Sgt. Jones told Sgt. Jimenez he didn't have his job anymore.

   _____

   _____

10. When the rioters left the buildings, the bystanders threw rocks at them.

   _____

   _____

CHAPTER FOUR   MECHANICS

Correct all capitalization errors in the following sentences.

1. The Witness said, "officer, I saw the red ford hit the pedestrian and get on the freeway going South."

2. Thomas said That he had seen the Burglar leaving Sam's market at 6 P.M.

3. the canine unit carried a German Shepherd.

4. Officers in the south believed the woman they were looking for had left georgia and was traveling toward the Northern part of the country.

5. Smithers, Vice President of Blue Dot inc., discovered the broken window when he arrived.

6. The grateful community awarded the Lieutenant the medal of valor after the riots last summer.

7. The juvenile said his Mom loaned him the mercedes but, "Boy, will dad be mad."

8. The bogus press newspaper quoted dr. Arnold, the Prime Suspect, as saying He got his idea from reading the Book *the bloody hatchet*.

9. The student told Officers the victim, ms. Rodriguez, taught biology II on tuesday and thursday, but he didn't know what other Science courses she taught.

10. To get to the Police Station, turn left off highway 62, go North on elm st. for two blocks, and then turn Right at the corner of elm and academy rd.

Insert periods, question marks, and/or exclamation marks in the following sentences.

1. The victim, Dr Ashcraft, reported the narcotics theft on Nov 10

2. Hurry The suspect just left

3. At the end of the interview, Sgt Bruckner asked if there was anything else she remembered

4. Is there anything else you can tell us about the accident

5. Go to the front door and wait for the lieutenant's instruction

Insert commas where necessary in these sentences.

1. You should tell Sergeant Merrill not Captain Greene about this.

2. I spoke to the victim and she said she had just returned home when she heard the sound of breaking glass.

3. After your preliminary investigation you may have to talk to some witnesses again.

4. The accident occurred on May 10 1989 in Denver Colorado.

5. Jenkins's suicide note referred to his relatives his depression his lack of success and his feelings of inadequacy.

6. While trying to escape the suspect tripped and fell.

7. Sergeant Washington is the prisoner in custody?

8. Mr. Blaney a neighbor said "I know I've seen the car before but I just can't remember where."

9. The address the suspect gave 101 North Regency Avenue Apt. C Juneau Alaska didn't exist.

10. The property somehow was stored in the chief's office rather than in the property room.

Add semicolons and colons to the following sentences.

1. He was supposedly extradited actually, he never left town.

2. The officer questioned three witnesses Lois Lane, the secretary Clark Kent, the reporter and Jimmy Olson, the copy boy.

3. Within three minutes of receiving the call, officers arrived however, the burglars were already gone.

4. After the alarm went off at 242 A.M., the thieves had only three minutes to finish the job and get out of the building.

5. Because the kidnappers were so inept, they wrote To Whom It May Concern on their ransom letter.

Add apostrophes and quotation marks to the following sentences.

1. They found the rare, first edition copy of Mark Twains story The Mysterious Stranger after ten years worth of searching.

2. The defense attorney asked, Isnt it true, Dr. Simpson, that you prescribed the medication?

3. Dont waste a second. The sergeant will go bonkers if were late.

4. The thieves took some mens clothes, two childrens bikes, and a womans diamond ring.

5. Officer Jacksons reports are always well written and punctual, but why does she use so many *thens*?

Add hyphens and dashes to the following sentences.

1. Woodall said his father in law caused the fight.

2. Deputies conducted a house to house search for the missing child.

3. About three fourths of the officers attended the meeting.

4. On pages 14 16 you will find the list of the twenty seven victims involved in the swindle.

5. He is the prime suspect the only suspect in the murder of the editor in chief of the newspaper.

Add parentheses, underlining, and periods (for ellipses) in the following sentences.

1. Tierney told officers he paid eighty dollars $80 for the counterfeit copy of the painting A Bowl of Cherries.

2. The jury foreman read the verdict: "We the jury in the case of the State versus Anthony Adverse on the charge of _____ find the defendant guilty."

3. Sometimes it is difficult to tell his i's from his e's.

4. Officers gave the citizen three options: 1 settle the disagreement calmly, 2 call his lawyer, or 3 sign a formal complaint.

5. Dr. Cole Slab what an appropriate name for a medical doctor said the unidentified victim was DOA dead on arrival.

Circle the correct usage of numbers in the following sentences.

1. Narcotics officers confiscated approximately (15/fifteen) pounds of cocaine.

2. They also logged into evidence ($15,863/fifteen thousand eight hundred sixty-three dollars) found at the scene.

3. (7/Seven) suspects were arraigned on various charges.

4. The youngest suspect was (18/eighteen) years old, and the oldest suspect was (62/sixty-two).

5. Investigators estimated the confiscated drugs represented only (25/twenty-five) percent of the total amount shipped to the suspect.

CHAPTER FIVE SPELLING

Make the following words plural.

woman _____   crash _____

patch _____   building _____

thief _____   deer _____

tattoo _____   foot _____

fireman _____   city _____

Add the suffixes -ed and -ing to the following words.

confer _____   quarrel _____

occur _____   hop _____

burglarize _____   begin _____

step _____   copy _____

accelerate _____   testify _____

Add -able to the following words.

agree _____   change _____

read _____   train _____

regret _____

Add -ness to the following words.

close _____   sad _____

happy _____   same _____

sick _____

Circle the correctly spelled words from the following choices.

aggravated   agravated   aggrevated

argumentive   argumentative   argumentative

cematery   cemetary   cemetery

disturbance	disturbence	disterbance
lewtenant	lieutenent	lieutenant
payed	payd	paid
proceedure	procedur	procedure
simular	similar	similiar
unconscious	unconsious	unconscience
writting	writeing	writing

Circle the correct homonym in each of the following sentences.

1. The (affect, effect) of the medication began to (affect, effect) his judgment.

2. Murder is a (capital, capitol) offense.

3. Investigators were (ceiling, sealing) the building when the (ceiling, sealing) caved in.

4. They could not (elicit, illicit) any answer from the man about his (elicit, illicit) gambling habits.

5. The point of entry was the (hole, whole) in the roof.

6. He felt (pain, pane) in his hand after he broke the (pain, pane).

7. That recruit's (principal, principle) fault is not being able to think clearly under pressure.

8. Hammerfield said he was (threw, through) arguing and (threw, through) the bottle at Martinez.

9. He was (to, too, two) slow (to, too, two) load the last (to, too, two) rounds in the shotgun.

10. (Your, You're) letter of commendation proves (your, you're) an exemplary officer.

CHAPTER SIX   POLICE REPORTS

Circle the correct answer for each of the following sentences.

1. The definition of a report is:
   a. Any documentation on a departmental form.
   b. Only documentation that is signed by a victim.
   c. Only documentation of crimes and not other events.

2. An arrest report must include:
   a. The chain of evidence.
   b. A request for forensic examination of evidence.
   c. Probable cause to stop, detain, and arrest the suspect.

3. Crime reports are completed:
   a. Only when you've recovered the stolen property.
   b. When your preliminary investigation concludes a crime has been committed.
   c. Because you need to document your daily activity.

4. Supplemental reports are completed:
   a. To record information you discover after the original report has been filed.
   b. To record the amount of time you've spent on the investigation.
   c. To record the number of similar crimes in the same area.

5. Police reports are written:
   a. To document criminal investigations.
   b. To provide reference material and historical data
   c. Both A and B.

6. The source documents for crime analysis are:
   a. Crime reports.
   b. Memorandums.
   c. Daily activity reports.

7. The report writing audience is made up of:
   a. Only police officers from your agency.
   b. Police officers, judges, administrators, and the media.
   c. Only those people directly at the scene of the crime.

8. The definition of accuracy in police reports is:
   a. Correct spelling and grammar.
   b. Use of correct report form.
   c. Exact conformity to fact, errorless.

9. The definition of clear in police reports is:
   a. Plain or evident to the mind of the reader.
   b. Understandable to anyone with an eighth-grade education.
   c. Using terms common to law enforcement professionals.

10. Concise in a police report means:
    a. Short and to the point.
    b. Less than one handwritten page.
    c. Saying as much as possible in as few words as possible.

CHAPTER SEVEN   REPORT WRITING TECHNIQUES

Deadwood Words

Replace each of the following words or phrases with a simple word or phrase.

1. at the present time   _____

2. contacted   _____

3. in the event of   _____

4. for the reason that   _____

5. during the course of   _____

6. a limited quantity of   _____

7. contingent upon receipt of _____

8. render aid or assistance   _____

9. due to the fact that   _____

10. ameliorate   _____

Word Meanings and Usage

Circle the correct word in the parentheses for each sentence.

1. The officers told Higgins they would (cite/site/sight) him if he came on the construction (cite/site/sight) again.

2. The attorney wondered if the drunk would be a (credible/creditable) witness.

3. The motorist was stranded in the (desert/dessert).

4. Don't (loose/lose) sight of the suspects.

5. The (nosey/noisy) neighbor complained about the party.

6. The suspect became (quiet/quit/quite) when the witness identified her.

7. Stolen cars are often (stripped/striped) before anyone finds them.

8. Rodriguez (waived/waved) his rights and confessed.

9. We (were/where) working in an area (wear/where) we had to (where/wear) special uniforms.

10. The officers had (all ready/already) arrived before the burglars were (all ready/already) to leave.

Revise the following sentences so they are clear, concise, and jargon- and slang-free.

1. The witness indicated to the investigating officer that she had in-deed observed the suspected culprit depart from the jewelry store just prior to the time that the officers responded to the location.

   _____

   _____

2. The assault victim was transported to the hospital where slides were taken of his head which was booked as evidence at the station.

   _____

   _____

3. Officer Kim searched the trunk with negative results.

   _____

   _____

4. The victim, Sally Shields, was really shook, but she was still cool about the details of what had gone down.

   _____

   _____

5. The neighbors were of the opinion that the investigators had left no stone unturned in the relentless search for the fugitive from justice.

   _____

   _____

6. Upon her arrival, Officer Beckworth ascertained that there were seven witnesses she had to contact in order to commence her investigation into the physical altercation between Samuels and Whitson.

   _____

   _____

7. Bound, gagged, and trussed up in a denim bag, with plugs in her ears and tape over her eyes, the victim Miss Sarah Sharp told yesterday how she was kidnapped.

   _____

   _____

8. She was brought down to the station by Detective Jorgenson for the purpose of the identification of the suspect.

   _____

   _____

9. The gang was made up of six Gray Devils from Frisco, an equal number of representatives from Sacramento, and the same amount of members from L.A.

   _____

   _____

10. Olson was verbally advised by this officer to give this officer the baton belonging to said officer.

    _____

    _____

Change the following passive-voice sentences to active-voice sentences.

1. Latent fingerprints were found on the empty bottle.

   _____

   _____

2. The monthly crime report was completed by Chief Bowman and submitted to the City Council.

   _____

   _____

3. Officer Charles was informed by Sgt. Lasiter that the search of the scene had been conducted by the laboratory technicians.

   _____

   _____

4. The juvenile suspect was found crouching behind some garbage cans in the alley by Officer Owens.

   _____

   _____

5. It was determined by the officers that entrance was gained by the burglars through a side door.

   _____

   _____

LIST OF IRREGULAR VERBS

Present	Past	Past Participle
are (is)	were (was)	been
bear	bore	borne
beat	beat	beaten
become	became	become
begin	began	begun
bend	bent	bent
bet	bet	bet
bid (offer)	bid	bid
bid (command)	bade	bidden
bite	bit	bitten
bleed	bled	bled
blow	blew	blown
break	broke	broken
bring	brought	brought
build	built	built
burst	burst	burst
buy	bought	bought
can	could	no past participle
cast	cast	cast
catch	caught	caught
choose	chose	chosen
cling	clung	clung
come	came	come
cost	cost	cost
creep	crept	crept
cut	cut	cut
deal	dealt	dealt
dive	dove/dived	dived
do (does)	did	done
draw	drew	drawn
drink	drank	drunk
drive	drove	driven
eat	ate	eaten
fall	fell	fallen
feed	fed	fed
feel	felt	felt
fight	fought	fought
find	found	found
flee	fled	fled
fling	flung	flung
fly (flies)	flew	flown
forget	forgot	forgot (-ten)
forgive	forgave	forgiven
freeze	froze	frozen
get	got	got/gotten
give	gave	given
go (goes)	went	gone

Present	*Past*	*Past Participle*
grind	ground	ground
grow	grew	grown
hang	hung	hung
have (has)	had	had
hear	heard	heard
hide	hid	hidden
hit	hit	hit
hold	held	held
hurt	hurt	hurt
keep	kept	kept
know	knew	known
lay	laid	laid
lead	led	led
leave	left	left
lend	lent	lent
let	let	let
lie	lay	lain
lose	lost	lost
make	made	made
may	might	no past participle
mean	meant	meant
meet	met	met
pay	paid	paid
put	put	put
quit	quit	quit
read	read	read
rid	rid	rid
ride	rode	ridden
ring	rang	rung
rise	rose	risen
run	ran	run
say	said	said
see	saw	seen
seek	sought	sought
sell	sold	sold
send	sent	sent
set	set	set
shake	shook	shaken
shed	shed	shed
shine	shone	shone
shoot	shot	shot
shrink	shrank	shrunk
shut	shut	shut
sing	sang	sung
sink	sank/sunk	sunk
sit	sat	sat
sleep	slept	slept
slide	slid	slid
slit	slit	slit

Present	*Past*	*Past Participle*
speak	spoke	spoken
speed	sped	sped
spend	spent	spent
spin	spun	spun
split	split	split
spread	spread	spread
spring	sprang/sprung	sprung
stand	stood	stood
steal	stole	stolen
sting	stung	stung
strike	struck	struck
swear	swore	sworn
sweep	swept	swept
swim	swam	swum
swing	swung	swung
take	took	taken
teach (teaches)	taught	taught
tear	tore	torn
tell	told	told
think	thought	thought
throw	threw	thrown
thrust	thrust	thrust
wear	wore	worn
weave	wove	woven
win	won	won
wind	wound	wound
write	wrote	written

Note: Of is never a helping verb. If you have ever said or written, "I could *of* done it," you meant, "I could *have* done it."

LIST OF NONACTION LINKING VERBS

is	may	has
are	can	had
was	must	will
were	could	shall
am	would	might
be	should	look
been	do	feel
being	does	seem
become	did	taste
became	have	appear

PRACTICE SCENARIOS AND SAMPLE REPORTS

Directions: Write an appropriate narrative for each of the following scenarios. If you are using police department crime reports, complete all necessary portions of the form. If necessary, use today's date and time. You are the officer assigned to take the report. Include your actions as the investigating officer.

Scenario 1 Bicycle Theft Report

You are sent to 14621 Spring Street, Riverdale, to take a bicycle theft report. Your reporting party/victim is:

Victim:	Sheila Marie Garvin DOB: 1-18-70
Phones:	(h) 891-1722 (w) 835-3802
Work Address:	212 North Main St., Corona, CA 92000
Occupation:	Office Manager Female-Caucasian

You interview Ms. Garvin and she tells you the following: She took her 10-year-old son to school at 7:45 A.M. She remembers seeing the bicycle in the driveway because her son had to move it out of the way. He put the bicycle on the front porch. After she took him to school, she stopped at the grocery store to buy some milk. She returned home at approximately 8:30 A.M.

When she got home, the bicycle was gone. She looked in the rear yard and garage but couldn't find it. No one has permission to use the bicycle.

She described the bicycle as a boy's 26-inch Huffy All American, painted red and white, with a black seat. She paid $185 for it.

Scenario 2 Minor in Possession of Alcohol

You park your police car and walk through Mt. Rushmore City Park, located at the corner of Park Drive and Mountain Avenue. It is a violation of city ordinance No. 3-18 to possess alcoholic beverages in a city park, and it is also a violation of state law for a minor (someone between the ages of eighteen and twenty-one years) to possess an alcoholic beverage.

You walk toward the outdoor handball courts and see a young male subject sitting on the ground. He's got a can of Budweiser beer in his right hand. When you walk up to him, he tries to hide it behind his right leg.

At your request, the subject gives you his driver's license and hands you the can of beer. He admits it is his. His driver's license shows that he is only 19 years old.

You dump out the liquid in the can to make sure it looks and smells like beer. You arrest him for possession of an alcoholic beverage by a minor and release him on a citation at the scene.

Suspect:	James Michael Senecal DOB: 12-5-___
Phones:	(h) 981-7122

| Home Address: | 1012 Marigold, Middletown, USA |
| Occupation: | Unemployed Male-Caucasian |

Scenario 3 Residential Burglary

You are sent to 24906 Mayberry Road, Hometown, to take a residential burglary report. Your reporting party/victim is:

Victim:	Allen Mark Talbot DOB: 2-23-49
Phones:	(h) 918-1227 (w) 235-0242
Work Address:	1039 Broadway, Hometown, CA 90000
Occupation:	Engineer Male-Caucasian

Talbot locked all the windows and doors to his house and left for work at 7:45 this morning. He came home at about 5:30 P.M. and found the front door open. When he went inside, he discovered someone had torn his house apart. The furniture was overturned, drawers were emptied on the floor, and clothes were removed from the closet.

He checked the dresser in the master bedroom and found approximately three hundred dollars in cash missing. He also found his Rolex watch was missing from the night table by his bed.

You check the residence to find physical evidence and the point of entry. You find the sliding glass door to the master bedroom has been pried open and there's a small screwdriver left on the patio. You check the neighborhood for witnesses and can't find anyone who saw the suspect.

Mr. Talbot lives alone since his wife died two years ago, and he doesn't have any idea who broke into his house.

SAMPLE REPORTS

Petty Theft

Victim Garcia left for work this morning at 7:30 A.M. He remembered seeing his potted plant on the front porch next to the door. When he came home for lunch at 12:30 P.M., the plant was gone. He didn't have any idea who took the plant.

Assault and Battery

Today at 4:50 P.M., Deputy Arzate and I were dispatched to a report of 2 men fighting at the Sip-n-Bull Bar. When we arrived, Laughlin and Lindstrom were fighting outside the bar. Arzate and I separated the 2 men, and I interviewed Laughlin first. Deputy Arzate stayed with Lindstrom.

Laughlin told me the following: He and Lindstrom met in the bar about 6 months ago. They usually meet there about twice a week, especially during the football season. Laughlin said they make "friendly" wagers on the upcoming games. In the past 2 weeks, Laughlin has won $250 from Lindstrom, but Lindstrom hasn't paid his debt.

Today they started drinking beer about 2:00 P.M. and talking about this week's games. When Laughlin asked Lindstrom to pay him, they began to argue. Finally, Lindstrom pushed Laughlin off the bar stool. When Laughlin got up, Lindstrom used his right hand in a clenched fist to punch Laughlin in the face. The punch knocked Laughlin to the floor.

Laughlin said he was afraid of Lindstrom. He got up and ran out of the bar, but Lindstrom caught him outside. Laughlin said the police arrived at about the same time.

I explained private person arrest to Laughlin, and he said he was willing to arrest Lindstrom.

I walked up to Lindstrom and said, "How's it going?" Lindstrom spontaneously said, "I'm sorry. I shouldn't have punched his lights out. I know I owe him the money, but I've been out of work for 2 months." When I told Lindstrom that Laughlin was going to arrest him, Lindstrom said, "I won't cause you any trouble. I've been arrested before."

Laughlin arrested Lindstrom for assault and battery. I handcuffed Lindstrom and booked him at the county jail.

Residential Burglary

I interviewed victim Brower and she told me the following: At 7:30 A.M. she left her house and was sure all windows and doors were locked. She returned at 9:30 A.M. and unlocked the front door to let herself into the house.

She saw the TV and stereo were missing from the living room, but nothing else in the house was disturbed. She went into the kitchen and saw the rear door was open. She didn't see any signs of forced entry or damage to the door. Ms. Brower said she didn't have any idea who broke into her house.

I called for an identification technician to check for latent fingerprints and other physical evidence.

When I left the residence, a neighbor and witness, Mrs. White, came up and told me what she saw. Her house is across the street, and from her kitchen window she can see the front of Brower's residence.

White said she saw 2 men sitting in a small pickup truck in front of Brower's house at about 8:30 A.M. The 2 men talked for a while; then the older one got out of the driver's door and went around to the back of Brower's house. In a few minutes, he came out the front door carrying the television. He put the TV in the back of the truck. The second man got out of the truck and went through the front door into the house and came out with the stereo. He got in the cab of the truck with the stereo. The older man was already in the driver's seat. The men drove north toward Vineyard Road.

White said she didn't recognize the men or the truck but could identify both men and the truck if she saw them again.

Garage Burglary

When I arrived, I spoke to McNeal in the garage of her home. She told me she came home from the bank about 11:30. A.M. She parked her car in the garage, left her purse on the front seat, and went inside her house. The car was unlocked and the garage was open. She came out to her car at 11:50 A.M. and her purse was gone.

While checking the neighborhood for witnesses, I found McNeal's purse in the Pollastro's front yard, under a bush next to the driveway. I talked to Pollastro, and she told me she saw the suspect walking down the sidewalk at about 11:35 A.M. The suspect walked up McNeal's driveway toward the garage. Pollastro did not see him go into the garage, and that was the last Pollastro saw him. Pollastro thought she could identify the suspect if she saw him again.

I returned the purse to McNeal. She looked through it and said the only thing missing was cash.

Armed Robbery

At 1550 hours, I was dispatched to an armed robbery that just occurred at Bob's Liquor Store. I arrived at 1553 hours and met Gene Senecal in the parking lot. He was very excited and told me the suspect vehicle just left w/b on Los Alisos toward the freeway.

I radioed the information to the Sheriff's Department Dispatcher, who initiated a general broadcast to all county law enforcement personnel.

Senecal told me he was working as a clerk at the front counter when the suspect entered the store alone. The suspect walked to the rear cooler, returned with a bottle of wine, and set it on the counter. The suspect took a small, shiny handgun from his waistband, pointed at Senecal, and said, "Gimme all the money."

Senecal took about a hundred dollars from the register and gave it to the suspect. The suspect took a white Michelle's Donut Shop paper bag from his pocket and put the money inside. The suspect ran out the front door, touching the glass door near the height marker with his hand as he left.

The suspect got into a light blue VW Bug and drove out of the lot w/b on Los Alisos. Senecal ran outside, wrote the license plate number on a piece of paper, and went back inside to call the police. Senecal said he could identify the suspect.

Witness Alvarez said he was stocking the cooler in the rear of the store when the suspect approached him, asking where the wine was. Alvarez told the suspect where the wine was and left the store to finish unloading a delivery truck.

I called the Watch C and asked for Crime Scene Investigation to respond. I collected the piece of paper with the license number on it and booked it into evidence locker #22.

Residential Burglary

Davis told me the following: He left his house at 7 P.M. and went to the movies. He returned home at 10:30 P.M. and found his front door open. He went inside and found his VCR and camcorder missing from the family room. He didn't look through the house any further but called the police.

I spoke to neighbor Jeffers, who told me the following: He saw the suspect walk across Davis's front yard at 8 P.M. The suspect was carrying a camcorder. He got into a white Chevrolet and drove away. He remembered the license plate started with 3DFG. Jeffers didn't have any additional information about the suspect or vehicle.

I checked the neighborhood for additional witnesses or evidence and didn't find anyone or anything.

At 11:00 P.M., I saw a car on Main Street matching the description and partial license plate number Jeffers had given me. I stopped the car, and while shining my flashlight through the driver's side rear window, I saw a camcorder matching the one taken in the Davis burglary. I asked the suspect to step out of the car and stand on the curb.

I arrested the suspect for burglary, handcuffed him, and put him in the backseat of my police car. His driver's license identified him as Richard Wilson. I Mirandized Wilson from my department-issued car. He said "Yes" he understood his rights and "Yes" he would talk to me about the crime.

Wilson told me he went to Davis's house at 8 P.M. He rang the doorbell, but no one answered. He twisted the doorknob off using vise grips, entered the house, and took the VCR and camcorder.

I searched Wilson's car and recovered both the VCR and camcorder. I returned both items to Davis.

I drove Wilson to the station and booked him for residential burglary.

Observation Arrest

While walking through Greenville Park, I saw Benson sitting on a park bench, smoking a marijuana cigarette. I confiscated the cigarette.

Benson admitted the marijuana cigarette was his. I wrote Benson a citation for the violation and booked the marijuana into evidence locker #58.

Theft Report

Brown told me the following: He went to the Cinemegaplex Movie Theatre, and the movie was over about 2:15 P.M. He rode straight home on his bicycle. When he got home, he left his bicycle on the front porch and went inside the house. When he came back outside about 30 minutes later, the bike was gone. No one had permission to take or use the bike.

I checked the neighborhood for witnesses and evidence and didn't find anyone or anything.

Shoplifter in Custody

I was dispatched to Short's Drug Store regarding a shoplifter in custody. When I arrived, one of the cashiers directed me to the upstairs security office and I met Senior Loss Prevention Agent Kennedy. Suspect Dunham was handcuffed behind his back and seated in a chair inside the office. I saw a camera, a wallet, and some keys sitting on the table in front of Dunham.

Kennedy told me he was in his security office watching the store through the two-way security glass. He saw Dunham enter the store alone through the north door at about 1 P.M. Dunham was walking slowly and constantly turning his head to look over both shoulders as if he were watching to see if anyone was watching him.

Dunham walked to the photo department, which is directly under Kennedy's office. He walked up to a floor display and picked up a camera with his right hand. He looked over both shoulders and placed the camera in his jacket pocket. He looked over both shoulders again and walked toward the exit. He walked past cash register #1, which was closed. Dunham walked out of the store through the north door. When Dunham got 15 feet outside the store, Kennedy approached him.

Kennedy identified himself verbally and with his security badge and arrested Dunham. Kennedy handcuffed Dunham and walked him back up to the security office. Kennedy searched Dunham and removed the camera from his right jacket pocket as well as a wallet and set of keys from Dunham's pants pockets. Kennedy agreed to retain the camera as evidence and signed a private person arrest form.

I read Dunham his Miranda rights from my department-issued card. He said he understood and waived his rights by answering "yes" and "yes" to the waiver questions. Dunham told me he came to the store to shop for a gift. He looked at the camera but wanted to look at something else also. There were no baskets around so he put the camera into his jacket pocket.

He walked toward the cash registers to ask a question, but all of the cashiers were busy. He decided to steal the camera and walked out of the store. When he got outside, Kennedy walked up to him, showing some kind of badge. Kennedy handcuffed him and walked him inside the store. Dunham said it was a mistake and offered to pay for the camera.

Dunham gave me permission to search his car so I did, but I didn't find any other stolen property. I cited and released Dunham.

Threatening Phone Call

I was dispatched to the Rawlings home regarding a threatening phone call. I arrived and spoke to Ron Rawlings, who told me he received the call about 8:00 P.M. last night. The suspect asked to speak to Ron's son John, who lives with Ron but who was not at home. The suspect asked Ron to pay him $1,000 to pay a debt John owed him. Ron asked the suspect why John owed him money, but the suspect refused to say.

Because the suspect would not say what the debt was for, Ron refused to pay. The suspect said, "I'm going to call you tomorrow morning and if you don't pay, I will gun down your whole family." Ron asked the suspect to identify himself, but the suspect hung up. When the suspect did not call this morning, Ron called the police. Ron did not recognize the voice but can identify it if he hears it again.

POLICE DEPARTMENT

REPORT

☐ NO PROSECUTION DESIRED
☐ INSURANCE REPORT
☐ COURTESY REPORT
☐ DOMESTIC VIOLENCE
☐ CONFIDENTIAL SEX CRIME

A ☐ ACTIVE
S ☐ SUSPENDED
R ☐ RECORDS
C ☐ CLOSED
K ☐ COURTESY
U ☐ UNFOUNDED

CASE NUMBER

REFER OTHER RPTS

INC. #

CRIME

CODE SECTION	CRIME		UCR CODE	SECONDARY-COUNTS	OTHER-COUNTS
SPECIFIC LOCATION OF CRIME		OCCURRED ON/OR BETWEEN:	DATE	DAY	TIME
BUSINESS NAME	DATE RPT'D TIME RPT'D	AND:	DATE	DAY	TIME

VICTIM

NAME (Last, First, Middle)	DL #		STATE	D.O.B.	SEX ☐ 1. M ☐ 2. F	RACE ☐ 1. WHT ☐ 2. HISP ☐ 3. BLK ☐ 5. CHI ☐ 7. FIL ☐ 9. P.ISL. ☐ 4. IND ☐ 6. JAP ☐ 8. OTH. ___
RESIDENCE ADDRESS		CITY	ZIP CODE		RES. PHONE ( )	
BUSINESS NAME AND ADDRESS/OCCUPATION		CITY	ZIP CODE		BUS. PHONE ( )	

VICTIM(S) - WITNESS - RP

CODE	NAME (Last, First, Middle)	DL #	STATE	D.O.B.	SEX ☐ 1. M ☐ 2. F	RACE ☐ 1. WHT ☐ 2. HISP ☐ 3. BLK ☐ 5. CHI ☐ 7. FIL ☐ 9. P.ISL. ☐ 4. IND ☐ 6. JAP ☐ 8. OTH. ___
	RESIDENCE ADDRESS		CITY	ZIP CODE	RES. PHONE ( )	
	BUSINESS NAME AND ADDRESS/OCCUPATION		CITY	ZIP CODE	BUS. PHONE ( )	
CODE	NAME (Last, First, Middle)	DL #	STATE	D.O.B.	SEX ☐ 1. M ☐ 2. F	RACE ☐ 1. WHT ☐ 2. HISP ☐ 3. BLK ☐ 5. CHI ☐ 7. FIL ☐ 9. P.ISL. ☐ 4. IND ☐ 6. JAP ☐ 8. OTH. ___
	RESIDENCE ADDRESS		CITY	ZIP CODE	RES. PHONE ( )	
	BUSINESS NAME AND ADDRESS/OCCUPATION		CITY	ZIP CODE	BUS. PHONE ( )	
CODE	NAME (Last, First, Middle)	DL #	STATE	D.O.B.	SEX ☐ 1. M ☐ 2. F	RACE ☐ 1. WHT ☐ 2. HISP ☐ 3. BLK ☐ 5. CHI ☐ 7. FIL ☐ 9. P.ISL. ☐ 4. IND ☐ 6. JAP ☐ 8. OTH. ___
	RESIDENCE ADDRESS		CITY	ZIP CODE	RES. PHONE ( )	
	BUSINESS NAME AND ADDRESS/OCCUPATION		CITY	ZIP CODE	BUS. PHONE ( )	

VIC VEH

LICENSE #	STATE	YEAR	MAKE	MODEL	BODY STYLE ☐ 0. UNK ☐ 2. 4-DR ☐ 4. P/U ☐ 6. VAN ☐ 8. RV ☐ 10. OTHER ☐ 1. 2-DR ☐ 3. CONV ☐ 5. TRUCK ☐ 7. S/W ☐ 9. M/C
COLOR/COLOR		OTHER CHARACTERISTICS (i.e. T/C Damage, Unique Marks or Paint, etc.)			DISPOSITION OF VEHICLE

FACTORS

☐ 1 THERE IS A WITNESS TO THE CRIME   SUSPECT PAGE ☐ YES ☐ NO
☐ 2 A SUSPECT WAS ARRESTED
☐ 3 A SUSPECT WAS NAMED
☐ 4 A SUSPECT CAN BE LOCATED
☐ 5 A SUSPECT CAN BE DESCRIBED
☐ 6 A SUSPECT CAN BE IDENTIFIED
☐ 7 A SUSPECT VEHICLE CAN BE IDENTIFIED
☐ 8 THERE IS IDENTIFIABLE STOLEN PROPERTY
☐ 9 THERE IS A SIGNIFICANT M.O.
☐ 10 SIGNIFICANT PHYSICAL EVIDENCE IS PRESENT
☐ 11 THERE IS A MAJOR INJURY/SEX CRIME INVOLVED
☐ 12 THERE IS A GOOD POSSIBILITY OF A SOLUTION
☐ 13 FURTHER INVESTIGATION NEEDED
☐ 14 CRIME IS GANG RELATED
☐ 15 HATE CRIME RELATED

EVIDENCE

☐ 0 NONE
☐ 1 FINGERPRINTS
☐ 2 TOOLS
☐ 3 TOOL MARKINGS
☐ 4 GLASS
☐ 5 PAINT
☐ 6 BULLET CASING
☐ 7 BULLET
☐ 8 RAPE KIT
☐ 9 SEMEN

☐ 10 BLOOD
☐ 11 URINE
☐ 12 HAIR
☐ 13 FIREARMS
☐ 14 PHOTOGRAPHS
☐ 15 OTHERS (DESCRIBE)

VICTIM'S SIGNATURE	DATE	DETECTIVE ASSIGNED	DATE

REPORTING OFFICER	ID#	DATE	REVIEWING SUPERVISOR	ID#	DATE

COPIES: ☐ CHIEF ☐ CAPT. ☐ PATROL ☐ DB ☐ CSI
TO: ☐ DMV ☐ CAU ☐ ABC (2 copies) ☐ DA ☐ OTHER ___

ROUTED BY

ENTERED BY

ERPD Form 2/99

PREMISES	POINT OF ENTRY	PROPERTY ATTACKED	SUSPECT(S) ACTIONS	SUSP. PRET. TO BE
BUSINESS	☐ 0 Unknown	☐ 0 Unknown	☐ 1 Alarm Disarmed	☐ 0 N/A
☐ 1 Bank/Sav Loan	☐ 0 N/A	☐ 0 N/A	☐ 2 Arson	☐ 1 Conducting Survey
Finance/Credit Un	☐ 1 Front	☐ 1 Cash Notes	☐ 3 Ate/Drank on Premises	☐ 2 Cust./Client
☐ 2 Bar	☐ 2 Rear	☐ 2 Clothes/Fur	☐ 4 Blindfolded Victim	☐ 3 Delivery Person
☐ 3 Cleaners/Laundry	☐ 3 Side	☐ 3 Consumable Goods	Bound/Gagged	☐ 4 Disabled Motorist
☐ 4 Construction Site	☐ 4 Door	☐ 4 Firearms	☐ 5 Cat Burglar	☐ 5 Drunk
☐ 5 Theater	☐ 5 Window	☐ 5 Household Goods	☐ 6 Defecated/Urinated	☐ 6 Employee/Employer
☐ 6 Fast Foods	☐ 6 Sliding Glass Door	☐ 6 Jewelry Metals	☐ 7 Demanded Money	☐ 7 Friend/Relative
☐ 7 Gas Station	☐ 7 Basement	☐ 7 Livestock	☐ 8 Disrobed Victim Fully	☐ 8 Ill/Injured
☐ 8 Hotel/Motel	☐ 8 Roof	☐ 8 Office Equipment	☐ 9 Disrobed Victim Partially	☐ 9 Need Phone
☐ 9 Dept./Discount Store	☐ 9 Floor	☐ 9 TV/Radio/Camera	☐ 10 Fired Weapon	☐ 10 Police/Law
☐ 10 Drug Store	☐ 10 Wall	☐ 10 Miscellaneous	☐ 11 Force Vic to Move	☐ 11 Renter
☐ 11 Gun/Sport Goods	☐ 11 Duct/Vent	☐ 11 other _____	☐ 12 Force Vic into Veh	☐ 12 Repairman
☐ 12 Jewelry Store	☐ 12 Garage		☐ 13 Has Been Drinking	☐ 13 Sale of Illicit Goods
☐ 13 Liquor Store	☐ 13 Adj. Building		☐ 14 Indication Multi Susps.	☐ 14 Sales Person
☐ 14 Photo Stand	☐ 14 Ground Level	**SEX CRIMES ONLY**	☐ 15 Inflicted Injuries	☐ 15 Seeking Assistance
☐ 15 Convenience Store	☐ 15 Upper Level	☐ 1 Suspect Climaxed	☐ 16 Knew Location of	☐ 16 Seeking Directions
☐ 16 Restaurant	☐ 16 Other _____	☐ 2 Unknown/Climaxed	Hidden Cash	☐ 17 Seeking Someone
☐ 17 Supermarket		☐ 3 Victim Bound/Tied	☐ 17 Made Threats	☐ 18 Solicit Funds
☐ 18 TV/Radio	**METHOD OF ENTRY**	☐ 4 Victim Injured	☐ 18 Place properties in	☐ 19 other _____
☐ 19 Auto Parts	☐ 0 Unknown	☐ 5 Covered Victim Face	Sack/Pocket	_____
☐ 20 Bicycle Sales	☐ 0 N/A	☐ 6 Photographed Victim	☐ 19 Prepared Exit	_____
☐ 21 Car/Motorcycle Sales	☐ 1 No Force Used	☐ 7 Vic Orally Copulated Susp	☐ 20 Ransacked	_____
☐ 22 Clothing Store	☐ 2 Attempt Only	☐ 8 Susp Orally Copulated Vic	☐ 21 Ripped/Cut Clothing	_____
☐ 23 Hardware	☐ 3 Bodily Force	☐ 9 Rape By Instrument	☐ 22 Selective in Loot	_____
☐ 24 Medical	☐ 4 Bolt Cut/Pliers	(Foreign Objects)	☐ 23 Shut Off Power	_____
☐ 25 Office Building	☐ 5 Channel Lock/Pipe	☐ 10 Sodomy	☐ 24 Smoked on Premises	_____
☐ 26 Shoe Store	Wrench/Vice Grips	☐ 11 Suggested Vic Commit	☐ 25 Searched Victim	
☐ 27 Warehouse	☐ 6 Saw/Drill/Burn	Lewd Perverted Act	☐ 26 Struck Victim	**PHYSICAL SECURITY**
☐ 28 other _____	☐ 7 Screwdriver	☐ 12 Inserted Finger Into Vagina	☐ 27 Susp Armed	☐ 0 Unknown
_____	☐ 8 Tire Iron	☐ 13 Forced Vic to Fondle Susp	☐ 28 Threatened Retaliation	☐ 0 N/A
	☐ 9 Unk Pry Bar	☐ 14 Susp Fondled Victim	☐ 29 Took Only Consumables	☐ 1 Audible Alarm
RESIDENCE	☐ 10 Coat Hanger Wire	☐ 15 Masturbated Self	☐ 30 Took Victim's Vehicle	☐ 2 Silent Alarm
☐ 29 Apartment	☐ 11 Key Slip Shim	☐ 16 other _____	☐ 31 Tortured	☐ 3 Private Security Patrol
☐ 30 Condominium	☐ 12 Punch	_____	☐ 32 Under Influence Drugs	☐ 4 Dog
☐ 31 Duplex/Fourplex	☐ 13 Remove Louvers		☐ 33 Used Demand Note	☐ 5 Standard Locks
☐ 32 Garage Attached	☐ 14 Window Smash	**BURGLARY ONLY**	☐ 34 Used Lookout	☐ 6 Auxiliary Locks
☐ 33 Garage Detached	☐ 15 Brick/Rock	Is member of Neigh Watch?	☐ 35 Used Driver	(Deadbolt Windows, etc.)
☐ 34 House	☐ 16 Hid in Building	☐ Yes ☐ No	☐ 36 Used Match/Candle	☐ 7 Window Bars/Grills
☐ 35 Mobile Home	☐ 17 Other _____	Is member of Operation Ident?	☐ 37 Used Victim's Name	☐ 8 Outside Lighting On
☐ 36 other _____		☐ Yes ☐ No	☐ 38 Used Victim's	☐ 9 Inside Lighting On
_____	**VEHICLE ENTRY**	Interested in NW?	Suitcase/Pillowcase	☐ 10 Garage Door Locked
	☐ 0 Unknown	☐ Yes ☐ No	☐ 39 Used Victim's Tools	☐ 11 Obscured Interior View
PUBLIC	☐ 0 N/A	Had Home Business Inspection?	☐ 40 Veh Needed to	(Commercial/Business)
☐ 37 Church	☐ 1 Door/Lock Forced	☐ Yes ☐ No	Remove Property	☐ 12 Security Signing
☐ 38 Hospital	☐ 2 Truck Forced	When? _____	☐ 41 Cut/Disconnected Phone	(N.W., Alarm, etc.)
☐ 39 Park/Playground	☐ 3 Window Broken _____	_____	☐ 42 Cased Location	☐ 13 other _____
☐ 40 Parking Lot	☐ 4 Window Forced _____	_____	Before Crime	_____
☐ 41 Public Building	☐ 5 Window Open _____		☐ 43 other _____	_____
☐ 42 School	☐ 6 Unlocked		_____	_____
☐ 43 Shopping Mall	☐ 7 other _____		_____	_____
☐ 44 Street/Hwy/Alley				
☐ 45 Other _____				

VEHICLE			**VICTIM PROFILE**		
☐ 46 Camper					
☐ 47 Motor Home	**PHYSICAL CONDITION**	**REALATIONSHIP TO SUSPECT**		**MARITAL STATUS**	
☐ 48 Passenger Car	☐ 0 No Impairment	☐ 0 Unknown	☐ 9 Other Family	☐ 0 Unknown	
☐ 49 Pick-up	☐ 1 Under Infl. Alcohol/Drugs	☐ 1 Husband	☐ 10 Acquaintance	☐ 1 Annulled	
☐ 50 Trailer	☐ 2 Sick/Injured	☐ 2 Wife	☐ 11 Friend	☐ 2 Common Law	
☐ 51 Truck	☐ 3 Senior Citizen	☐ 3 Mother	☐ 12 Boyfriend	☐ 3 Single	
☐ 52 Van	☐ 4 Blind	☐ 4 Father	☐ 13 Girlfriend	☐ 4 Married	
☐ 53 Other _____	☐ 5 Handicapped	☐ 5 Daughter	☐ 14 Neighbor	☐ 5 Divorced	
	☐ 6 Deaf	☐ 6 Son	☐ 15 Business Associate	☐ 6 Widow(er)	
	☐ 7 Mute	☐ 7 Brother	☐ 16 Stranger	☐ 7 Separated	
	☐ 8 Mentally/Emotionally Impaired	☐ 8 Sister	☐ 17 other _____	☐ 8 other _____	
	☐ 9 other _____				

POLICE DEPARTMENT   SUSPECT REPORT

CASE NUMBER

CRIME

CODE SECTION	CRIME		UCR CODE	REFER OTHER RPTS

LOCATION (Be Specific)	RD.	DATE	TIME	SUPPL. ☐	INC. #

SUSP. VEH

LICENSE #	STATE	YEAR	MAKE	MODEL	BODY STYLE

BODY STYLE: ☐ 0. UNK ☐ 2. 4-DR ☐ 4. P/U ☐ 6. VAN ☐ 8. RV ☐ 10. OTHER ☐ 1. 2-DR ☐ 3. CONV ☐ 5. TRUCK ☐ 7. S/W ☐ 9. M/C

COLOR/COLOR	OTHER CHARACTERISTICS (i.e. T/C Damage, Unique Marks or Paint, etc.)	DISPOSITION OF VEHICLE

REGISTERED OWNER

SUSPECT

SUSP. #	NAME (Last, First, Middle)	SEX ☐ 1. M ☐ 2. F	RACE

RACE: ☐ 0. UNK ☐ 2. HISP ☐ 4. IND ☐ 6. JAP ☐ 8. OTH _____ ☐ 1. WHT ☐ 3. BLK ☐ 5. CHI ☐ 7. FIL ☐ 9. P.ISL.

AKA	D.O.B.	AGE	HT.	WT.	BUILD

BUILD: ☐ 1. THIN ☐ 3. HEAVY ☐ 0. UNK ☐ 2. MED ☐ 4. MUSCLR

HAIR: ☐ 0. UNK ☐ 2. BLK ☐ 4. RED ☐ 6. S/P ☐ 8. OTHER ☐ 1. BRN ☐ 3. BLN ☐ 5. GRAY ☐ 7. WHT _____

EYES: ☐ 0. UNK ☐ 2. BLK ☐ 4. GRN ☐ 6. GRAY ☐ 1. BRN ☐ 3. BLU ☐ 5. HAZEL ☐ 7. OTHER _____

D.L. #

RESIDENCE ADDRESS	STATE	ZIP CODE	RES. PHONE # ( )	S.S. #

BUSINESS ADDRESS	STATE	ZIP CODE	BUS. PHONE # ( )	OCCUPATION

CLOTHING	ARRESTED ☐ 1. YES ☐ 2. NO	STATUS ☐ 1. DRIVER ☐ 3. PED ☐ 2. PASS	GANG AFFILIATION: HOW KNOWN:	☐ 1. KNOWN ☐ 2. SUSPECTED

AMT. OF HAIR	HAIR STYLE	COMPLEXION	TATTOOS/SCARS	WEAPON(S)
☐ 0 UNKNOWN	☐ 0 UNKNOWN	☐ 0 UNKNOWN	☐ 0 UNKNOWN ☐ 0 NONE	☐ 0 UNKNOWN ☐ 0 NONE
☐ 1 THICK	☐ 1 LONG	☐ 1 CLEAR	☐ 1 FACE _____	☐ 1 CLUB _____
☐ 2 THIN	☐ 2 SHORT	☐ 2 ACNE	☐ 2 TEETH _____	☐ 2 HAND GUN _____
☐ 3 RECEDING	☐ 3 COLLAR	☐ 3 POCKED	☐ 3 NECK _____	☐ 3 OTHER UNK GUN _____
☐ 4 BALD	☐ 4 MILITARY	☐ 4 FRECKLED	☐ 4 R/ARM _____	☐ 4 RIFLE _____
☐ 5 OTHER _____	☐ 5 CREW CUT	☐ 5 WEATHERED	☐ 5 L/ARM _____	☐ 5 SHOT GUN _____
TYPE OF HAIR	☐ 6 RIGHT PART	☐ 6 ALBINO	☐ 6 R/HAND _____	☐ 6 TOY GUN _____
☐ 0 UNKNOWN	☐ 7 LEFT PART	☐ 7 OTHER _____	☐ 7 L/HAND _____	☐ 7 SIMULATED _____
☐ 1 STRAIGHT	☐ 8 CENTER PART	**GLASSES**	☐ 8 R/LEG _____	☐ 8 POCKET KNIFE _____
☐ 2 CURLY	☐ 9 STRAIGHT BACK	☐ 0 UNKNOWN	☐ 9 L/LEG _____	☐ 9 BUTCHER KNIFE _____
☐ 3 WAVY	☐ 10 PONY TAIL	☐ 0 NONE	☐ 10 R/SHOULDER _____	☐ 10 OTH. CUT/STAB INST _____
☐ 4 FINE	☐ 11 AFRO/NATURAL	☐ 1 YES (No Descrip.)	☐ 11 L/SHOULDER _____	☐ 11 HANDS/FEET _____
☐ 5 COARSE	☐ 12 PROCESSED	☐ 2 REG GLASSES	☐ 12 FRONT TORSO _____	☐ 12 BODILY FORCE _____
☐ 6 WIRY	☐ 13 TEASED	☐ 3 SUN GLASSES	☐ 13 BACK TORSO _____	☐ 13 STRANGULATION _____
☐ 7 WIG	☐ 14 OTHER _____	☐ 4 WIRE FRAME	☐ 14 OTHER _____	☐ 14 TIRE IRON _____
☐ 8 OTHER _____	**FACIAL HAIR**	☐ 5 PLASTIC FRAME		☐ 15 OTHER _____
HAIR CONDITION	☐ 0 UNKNOWN	☐ Color _____	**UNIQUE CLOTHING** / **WEAPON IN**	**WEAPON FEATURE**
☐ 0 UNKNOWN	☐ 0 N/A	☐ 6 OTHER _____	☐ 0 UNK ☐ 0 NONE / ☐ 0 UNKNOWN	☐ 0 UNKNOWN ☐ 0 NONE
☐ 1 CLEAN	☐ 1 CLN SHAVEN	**VOICE**	☐ 1 CAP/HAT / ☐ 0 N/A	☐ 1 ALTERED STOCK _____
☐ 2 DIRTY	☐ 2 MOUSTACHE	☐ 0 UNKNOWN	_____ / ☐ 1 BAG/BRIEFCASE	☐ 2 SAWED OFF _____
☐ 3 GREASY	☐ 3 FULL BEARD	☐ 0 N/A	☐ 2 GLOVES / ☐ 2 NEWSPAPER	☐ 3 AUTOMATIC _____
☐ 4 MATTED	☐ 4 GOATEE	☐ 1 LISP	_____ / ☐ 3 POCKET	☐ 4 BOLT ACTION _____
☐ 5 ODOR	☐ 5 FUMANCHU	☐ 2 SLURRED	☐ 3 SKI MASK / ☐ 4 SHOULDER	☐ 5 PUMP _____
☐ 6 OTHER _____	☐ 6 LOWER LIP	☐ 3 STUTTER	_____ / HOLSTER	☐ 6 REVOLVER _____
R/L HANDED	☐ 7 SIDE BURNS	☐ 4 ACCENT	☐ 4 STOCKING MASK / ☐ 5 WAISTBAND	☐ 7 BLUE STEEL _____
☐ 0 UNKNOWN	☐ 8 FUZZ	Describe _____	_____ / ☐ 6 OTHER _____	☐ 8 CHROME/NICKEL _____
☐ 1 RIGHT	☐ 9 UNSHAVEN	_____	☐ 5 OTHER _____	☐ 9 DOUBLE BARREL _____
☐ 2 LEFT	☐ 10 OTHER _____	☐ 5 OTHER _____		☐ 10 SINGLE BARREL _____
				☐ 11 OTHER _____

REPORTING OFFICER	ID#	DATE	REVIEWING SUPERVISOR	ID#	DATE

COPIES: TO:	☐ CHIEF ☐ CAPT ☐ PATROL ☐ DB ☐ CSI ☐ DMV ☐ CAU ☐ ABC (2 copies) ☐ DA ☐ OTHER _____	ROUTED BY	ENTERED BY

ESPD Form #200 (Rev 3/99)

CASE NO.	
	PAGE _____

SUSPECT

SUSP. #	NAME (Last, First, Middle)		SEX ☐ 1. M ☐ 2. F	RACE ☐ 0. UNK ☐ 1. WHT	☐ 2. HISP ☐ 3. BLK	☐ 4. IND ☐ 5. CHI	☐ 6. JAP ☐ 7. PIL	☐ 8. OTH _____ ☐ 9. P.ISL.

AKA	D.O.B.	AGE	HT.	WT.	BUILD ☐ 1. THIN ☐ 3. HEAVY ☐ 0. UNK ☐ 2. MED ☐ 4. MUSCLR

HAIR ☐ 0. UNK ☐ 2. BLK ☐ 4. RED ☐ 6. S/P ☐ 8. OTHER _____ ☐ 1. BRN ☐ 3. BLN ☐ 5. GRAY ☐ 7. WHT	EYES ☐ 0. UNK ☐ 2. BLK ☐ 4. GRN ☐ 6. GRAY ☐ 1. BRN ☐ 3. BLU ☐ 5. HAZEL ☐ 7. OTHER _____	D.L. #

RESIDENCE ADDRESS	STATE	ZIP CODE	RES. PHONE # ( )	S.S. #

BUSINESS ADDRESS (School)	STATE	ZIP CODE	BUS. PHONE # ( )	OCCUPATION

CLOTHING	ARRESTED ☐ 1. YES ☐ 2. NO	STATUS ☐ 1. DRIVER ☐ 3. PED ☐ 2. PASS	GANG AFFILIATION: HOW KNOWN:	☐ 1. KNOWN ☐ 2. SUSPECTED

AMT. OF HAIR	HAIR STYLE	COMPLEXION	TATTOOS/SCARS	DISTING. MARKS	WEAPON(S)
☐ 0 UNKNOWN	☐ 0 UNKNOWN	☐ 0 UNKNOWN	☐ 0 UNKNOWN	☐ 0 NONE	☐ 0 UNKNOWN ☐ 0 NONE
☐ 1 THICK	☐ 1 LONG	☐ 1 CLEAR	☐ 1 FACE _____		☐ 1 CLUB _____
☐ 2 THIN	☐ 2 SHORT	☐ 2 ACNE	☐ 2 TEETH _____		☐ 2 HAND GUN _____
☐ 3 RECEDING	☐ 3 COLLAR	☐ 3 POCKED	☐ 3 NECK _____		☐ 3 OTHER UNK GUN _____
☐ 4 BALD	☐ 4 MILITARY	☐ 4 FRECKLED	☐ 4 R/ARM _____		☐ 4 RIFLE _____
☐ 5 OTHER_____	☐ 5 CREW CUT	☐ 5 WEATHERED	☐ 5 L/ARM _____		☐ 5 SHOT GUN _____
TYPE OF HAIR	☐ 6 RIGHT PART	☐ 6 ALBINO	☐ 6 R/HAND _____		☐ 6 TOY GUN _____
☐ 0 UNKNOWN	☐ 7 LEFT PART	☐ 7 OTHER_____	☐ 7 L/HAND _____		☐ 7 SIMULATED _____
☐ 1 STRAIGHT	☐ 8 CENTER PART	**GLASSES**	☐ 8 R/LEG _____		☐ 8 POCKET KNIFE _____
☐ 2 CURLY	☐ 9 STRAIGHT BACK	☐ 0 UNKNOWN	☐ 9 L/LEG _____		☐ 9 BUTCHER KNIFE _____
☐ 3 WAVY	☐ 10 PONY TAIL	☐ 0 NONE	☐ 10 R/SHOULDER _____		☐ 10 OTH. CUT/STAB INST _____
☐ 4 FINE	☐ 11 AFRO/NATURAL	☐ 1 YES (No Descrip.)	☐ 11 L/SHOULDER _____		☐ 11 HANDS/FEET _____
☐ 5 COARSE	☐ 12 PROCESSED	☐ 2 REG GLASSES	☐ 12 FRONT TORSO _____		☐ 12 BODILY FORCE _____
☐ 6 WIRY	☐ 13 TEASED	☐ 3 SUN GLASSES	☐ 13 BACK TORSO _____		☐ 13 STRANGULATION _____
☐ 7 WIG	☐ 14 OTHER_____	☐ 4 WIRE FRAME	☐ 14 OTHER _____		☐ 14 TIRE IRON _____
☐ 8 OTHER_____	**FACIAL HAIR**	☐ 5 PLASTIC FRAME	_____		☐ 15 OTHER _____
HAIR CONDITION	☐ 0 UNKNOWN	☐ 5 Color_____			**WEAPON FEATURE**
☐ 0 UNKNOWN	☐ 0 N/A	☐ 6 OTHER_____	**UNIQUE CLTHNG**	**WEAPON IN**	☐ 0 UNKNOWN ☐ 0 NONE
☐ 1 CLEAN	☐ 1 CLN SHAVEN	**VOICE**	☐ 0 UNK ☐ 0 NONE	☐ 0 UNKNOWN	☐ 1 ALTERED STOCK _____
☐ 2 DIRTY	☐ 2 MOUSTACHE	☐ 0 UNKNOWN	☐ 1 CAP/HAT	☐ 0 N/A	☐ 2 SAWED OFF _____
☐ 3 GREASY	☐ 3 FULL BEARD	☐ 0 N/A	_____	☐ 1 BAG/BRIEFCASE	☐ 3 AUTOMATIC _____
☐ 4 MATTED	☐ 4 GOATEE	☐ 1 LISP	☐ 2 GLOVES	☐ 2 NEWSPAPER	☐ 4 BOLT ACTION _____
☐ 5 ODOR	☐ 5 FUMANCHU	☐ 2 SLURRED	_____	☐ 3 POCKET	☐ 5 PUMP _____
☐ 6 OTHER_____	☐ 6 LOWER LIP	☐ 3 STUTTER	☐ 3 SKI MASK	☐ 4 SHOULDER HOLSTER	☐ 6 REVOLVER _____
R/L HANDED	☐ 7 SIDE BURNS	☐ 4 ACCENT			☐ 7 BLUE STEEL _____
☐ 0 UNKNOWN	☐ 8 FUZZ	Describe_____	☐ 4 STOCKING MASK	☐ 5 WAISTBAND	☐ 8 CHROME/NICKEL _____
☐ 1 RIGHT	☐ 9 UNSHAVEN	_____		☐ 6 OTHER_____	☐ 9 DOUBLE BARREL _____
☐ 2 LEFT	☐ 10 OTHER_____	☐ 5 OTHER_____	☐ 5 OTHER_____		☐ 10 SINGLE BARREL _____
					☐ 11 OTHER _____

_____

_____

_____

_____

_____

_____

_____

_____

ORANGE COUNTY JAIL
Santa Ana, California

☐ **EXPEDITE BOOKING**
☐ **MEDICAL BOOKING**
☐ **NORMAL BOOKING**
PRE-BOOKING RECORD

FOR JAIL USE ONLY   *PLEASE PRINT OR TYPE*

BOOKING NUMBER	RECEIVING OFFICER / #	DATE	HOUSING LOCATION	BOOKING DEPUTY / #

SUPPLEMENTAL WARRANTS	HOW MANY	CAUTIONARY CODES: ☐ ESC ☐ VIO ☐ SUI ☐ OTHER_____

BOOKING STATUS

☐ STREET BOOKING	☐ WARRANT	☐ COURT ORDER	☐ BOOK AND RELEASE	☐ ENROUTE
☐ QR/SELF	☐ QR/OR	☐ QR/TR - DATE:_____		☐ LINE UP
☐ COMMT -_____		☐ PC 853.6	☐ OTHER SPECIFY_____	

ARRESTING OR TRANSPORTING OFFICER COMPLETE   ARRESTING AGENCY

NAME: LAST	FIRST	MIDDLE	BIRTHDATE

A.K.A.

ADDITIONAL A.K.A.

ILL OR INJURED ☐ YES ☐ NO	TYPE OF ILLNESS OR INJURY	DRIVER'S LIC. NO.	STATE
JURISDICTION	WARRANT AND/OR CASE NUMBER	BAIL	

CHARGE 1	CHARGE 4
CHARGE 2	CHARGE 5
CHARGE 3	CHARGE 6

PLACE OF BIRTH	CITIZENSHIP	OCCUPATION	SOCIAL SECURITY NO.

SEX	RACE	HEIGHT	WEIGHT	HAIR	EYES	BUILD	COMPLEXION	MARITAL STATUS	TELEPHONE NO.

SCARS, MARKS, TATTOOS, AMPS

ADDRESS	CITY	STATE	ZIP
NEXT OF KIN: NAME	TELEPHONE NO.	RELATIONSHIP	
ADDRESS	CITY	STATE	ZIP
EMPLOYED BY	BUSINESS ADDRESS		

OFFICER'S ADDITIONAL INFORMATION/CHECK BOX IF YOU BELIEVE THE INMATE WILL REQUIRE SPECIAL MANAGEMENT.
☐ MEDICAL ☐ MENTAL ☐ INTOXICATED ☐ PROTECTIVE CUSTODY ☐ HIGH SECURITY ☐ OTHER

ARRESTING AGENCY NUMBER	DATE/TIME ARRESTED	ARRESTING OFFICER / #	DR NO./GRID

PERMISSION TO USE TELEPHONE AFTER ARREST   (Pursuant to Penal Code Section 851.5)

I have been given the opportunity to make three (3) FREE telephone calls within the LOCAL DIALING area, or at MY OWN EXPENSE if OUTSIDE the local dialing area.

RECORD OF TELEPHONE CALLS:

Telephone calls DESIRED_____   Telephone calls COMPLETED_____

Location_____   Date_____   Time_____

Witnessing Officer_____   Badge #_____   Agency_____

SIGNATURE_____

FO680-195.3 (J) (R 1/87) AJS-ROO.O

FILE

Health Care Agency
County of Orange, California
Correctional Medical Services

INTAKE SCREENING AND TRIAGE

Temp.# _____

Date/Time "IN"

Name: _____ Booking#: _____ DOB: _____ Sex: ☐ M ☐ F

STATEMENT OF BOOKING OFFICER

Does the arrestee appear to be under the influence of drugs or alcohol, disoriented, confused or have impaired level of consciousness, or injured in any way? ☐ Yes ☐ No

Comments: _____

Officer's Signature: _____ Department: _____ Date: _____

MEDICAL/MENTAL QUESTIONNAIRE

1. Do you have any of the following problems?

☐ Asthma	☐ ENT Problems	☐ Hernia	☐ Intestinal Disorders	☐ Seizures
☐ Back Injuries	☐ FX/Sprains	☐ HIV/AIDS	☐ Mental Problems	☐ STD
☐ Deformities	☐ Heart Trouble	☐ High Blood Pressure	☐ Psych. Hospital	☐ Tuberculosis
☐ Dental Problems			☐ Pregnant/Due Date _____	
☐ Diabetes	☐ Hepatitis: Type: _____ Date: _____		☐ Other: _____	
☐ Disease/Operations	☐ NKA ☐ Allergies: _____			
	☐ Bee Sting			

	Y	N
2. Are you taking or do you need to take any prescribed medications (including psychiatric, birth control pills)?		
3. Have you ever been treated for tuberculosis?		
4. Have you had a cough for more than three weeks with any of the following: fever, weight loss, fatigue, night sweats?		
5. Have you had a head injury/traffic accident or altercation in the past 72 hours?		
6. Are you an alcoholic? Date of last drink: / Any seizures or DTs? How much do you drink?		
7. Do you use any street drugs such as heroin, cocaine, methamphetamine, marijuana or any other drugs? Method: How much: Last use:		
8. Are you receiving methadone? ☐ Detox or ☐ Maintenance		
9. Do you have any rashes, cuts, boils, abscesses, or other skin diseases?		
10. Do you have any artificial limbs, braces, dentures, hearing aid, contact lenses or eyeglasses?		
11. Have you ever tried to harm yourself or take your own life? When:		
12. Are you thinking of harming yourself now?		
13. Are you currently receiving psychiatric treatment?		
14. Have you been a patient in a hospital within the last 3 months?		
15. Have you ever been treated at a Regional Center or diagnosed with developmental problems?		
16. Do you know of any medical reason why you cannot work in jail?		

TRIAGE DISPOSITION
☐ Acceptable for Booking
☐ Medical
☐ Refer to Mental Health
☐ OK to Transfer to: ☐ Theo Lacy   ☐ James Musick
☐ Refused Assessment (see Number 23)
☐ E.R. Reason:

WORK STATUS
☐ General
☐ Kitchen
☐ No Kitchen
☐ Lite Duty/No Kitchen
☐ No Work
☐ Hold for Follow-up/Recheck on:

	Y	N
NURSE OBSERVATION		

17. Are there any signs of alcohol/drug intoxication and/or withdrawal?

☐ Tremors ☐ Slurred Speech ☐ Poor Coordination ☐ Gooseflesh ☐ Lethargy ☐ Odor

18. Any obvious respiratory problems? ☐ Dyspnea ☐ Wheezing ☐ Tachypnea

19. Is the arrestee: ☐ Combative ☐ Verbally Abusive ☐ Agitated

20. Is the arrestee: ☐ Incoherent ☐ Disoriented ☐ Lethargic ☐ Inappropriate

21. Is the arrestee: ☐ Hypertalkative ☐ Non-Communicative ☐ Vague ☐ Unkempt

22. Language spoken other than English: ☐ Spanish ☐ Vietnamese ☐ Other

23. NURSE ASSESSMENT (Please elaborate on positive findings):

24. MENTAL HEALTH ASSESSMENT (To be completed by CMH when indicated):

25. PPD Information (**BJ ONLY**)

Last PPD Date: _____ Results: ☐ Neg. ☐ Pos. Where: _____

Date Given: _____ Given by: _____

Date Read: _____ mm: _____ Read by: _____

26. **TRIAGE VITAL SIGNS (AS INDICATED)**

Temp:_____ Pulse: _____ Resp: _____ B/P: _____

Glucometer:_____ SpO$_2$: _____ Pain Scale: (1-10) _____

Nurse's Signature: _____ Name Stamp: _____ Date: _____

HEALTH INVENTORY

27. **Female Inmates Only**

Have you given birth in the past year? ☐ Yes ☐ No Date: _____ HCG Done: ☐ Date: _____

How many pregnancies have you had? _____ ☐ Negative

How many live births? _____ ☐ Positive

Any vaginal discharge? ☐ Yes ☐ No

Any history of breast cancer? ☐ Yes ☐ No

28. Any change in your medical status? ☐ Yes ☐ No If yes, refer to RN

29. Family history of medical problems? ☐ Yes ☐ No Please list:

30. Teaching:

31. Vital Signs:

Temp: _____ Pulse: _____ Resp: _____ B/P: _____

HT: _____ WT: _____

Signature/Title: _____ Name Stamp: _____ Date: _____

MD/NP Signature: _____ Name Stamp: _____ Date: _____

I am not aware of any physical, medical, dental or mental condition that would prevent me from participating in the work program and I have answered all questions truthfully and completely to the best of my ability.

Inmate's Signature: _____ Date:

Print Inmate Name:

Received by JO

CRIME SUMMARY INFORMATION

PROBABLE CAUSE DECLARATION

BAIL SETTING INFORMATION

BOOKING NO.

ARRESTEE (LAST, FIRST, MIDDLE)

DOB

ADDRESS (RESIDENCE)

BOOKING CHARGES

SUPPL. HOLDS

DATE / TIME OF ARREST

36-HR. EXP. DATE / TIME

ARRESTING AGENCY

ARRESTING OFFICER(S)

FACTS ESTABLISHING ELEMENTS AND IDENTIFICATION OF DEFENDANT:

_____

_____

_____

_____

_____

_____

_____

_____

_____

_____

_____

[ ] SEE ATTACHED REPORTS, INCORPORATED HEREIN BY THIS REFERENCE

[1] WEAPON DESCRIPTION:_____

[2] VICTIM'S AGE:_____ VICTIM'S INJURIES: _____

[3] VALUE OF PROP.LOSS: $_____ TYPE OF PROP.: _____

[4] TYPE OF NARCOTICS:_____ QTY:_____

[5] WHOLESALE VALUE: $_____ STEET VALUE: $_____

I DECLARE UNDER PENALTY OF PERJURY THAT THE FOREGOING IS TRUE AND CORRECT TO THE BEST OF MY INFORMATION AND BELIEF.

EXECUTED ON_____ AT ORANGE COUNTY, CALIFORNIA, BY_____

         (DATE)   (SIGNATURE)

ON THE BASIS OF ☐ THE OFFICER'S DECLARATION ☐ REPORTS REVIEWED, I HEREBY DETERMINE THAT THERE ☐ IS
☐ IS NOT PROBABLE CAUSE TO BELIEVE THIS ARRESTEE HAS COMMITTED A CRIME.

_____ _____ _____
     (DATE)   (TIME)   (SIGNATURE OF A JUDICIAL OFFICER)

FINDINGS AND ORDER

I find that exigent or exceptional circumstances prevent the making of a probable cause determination within 36 hours of the arrest of the person described in page 1 of this form, for the following reasons:

_____

_____

_____

_____

_____

_____

_____

_____

_____

☐ and on the basis of attached reports/documents.

I therefore order that this arrestee's probable cause determination hearing be continued to

_____ or to the next court day after today, whichever is earlier.
(Date and Time)

_____   _____   _____
        (Date)   (Time)   (Signature of Judicial Officer)

DR _____/_____

SHERIFF'S DEPARTMENT, ORANGE COUNTY
Santa Ana, California

TO: Michael S. Carona, Sheriff-Coroner

PEOPLE OF THE STATE OF CALIFORNIA

ORDER OF ARREST
BY
PRIVATE PERSON

vs

_____
Defendant

You are hereby requested to take into custody the above named defendant who I have arrested, for the commission of a public offense in my presence, under authority of the Penal Code of the State of California.

I will further, in the interest of Justice, appear at the Department of the Sheriff in and for Orange County when summoned by Sheriff Investigators to swear to a complaint against said defendant, and will appear as a witness for the people in any subsequent action when my presence is necessary to the prosection of said defendant.

I understand that having started these proceedings, I must follow through as above state, and if I do not, I may be brought into Court by process so that the case may be properly disposed of.

Date _____ Time _____

_____
Signature of Arresting Party

Witnessed:_____ , Deputy

_____ , Deputy

Pat 7 (Rev. 07-99)

SHERIFF'S DEPARTMENT
ORANGE COUNTY
SANTA ANA, CALIFORNIA

MICHAEL S. CARONA, SHERIFF-CORONER

STATEMENT OF SUBJECT

3. OFFENSE	4. VICTIM
5. NAME OF SUBJECT	6. ADDRESS OF SUBJECT
7. LOCATION OF INTERVIEW	8. DATE AND TIME OF INTERVIEW

ADVISEMENT OF RIGHTS

1. You have the right to remain silent.
    ("Do you understand that?")

2. Anything you say may be used against you in court.
    ("Do you understand that?")

3. You have the right to an attorney before and during any questioning.
    ("Do you understand?")

4. If you cannot afford an attorney, one will be appointed for you before questioning if you wish.
    ("Do you understand that?")

After advisement of the Miranda Rights, the Deputy shall obtain an expressed waiver from the suspect, by asking:

Question: Can we talk about what happened?

Answer: (Quote)

The above advisement was read to subject _____

by Deputy _____ .

- -

STATEMENT OF SUBJECT

10. INVESTIGATING OFFICERS	REPORT BY	11. DATE OF REPORT	12. APPROVED

F0680-79.2 (R5-90) (RS)

SHERIFF'S DEPARTMENT
ORANGE COUNTY
SANTA ANA, CALIFORNIA

2. Case No. _____

MICHAEL S, CARONA, SHERIFF-CORONER   **STATEMENT OF SUBJECT**

3. OFFENSE	4. VICTIM
5. NAME OF SUBJECT	6. ADDRESS OF SUBJECT
7. LOCATION OF INTERVIEW	8. DATE AND TIME OF INTERVIEW

AVISO DE MIRANDA

1. USTED TIENE EL DERECHO DE NO DECIR NADA.
   ENTIENDE?

2. LO QUE USTED DIGA AHORA SE PUEDE USAR, EN SU CONTRA EN UN TRIBUNAL.
   ENTIENDE?

3. USTED TIENE EL DERECHO A UN ABOGADO, ANTES Y DURANTE CUAL QUIER
   INTERROGATORIO.   ENTIENDE?

4. SI USTED NO TIENE DINERO PARA PAGAR PO UN ABOGADO, UNO LE SERA
   NOMBRADO ANTES CAULQUIER INTERROGATORIO, SI USTED LO DESEA.
   ENTIENDE?

After advisement of the Miranda Rights, the Deputy shall obtain an expressed waiver from the
suspect, by asking:

Question: DESEA HABLAR CONMIGO AHORA?

Answer: (Quote)

The above advisement was read to subject _____
by Deputy _____ .

- -

STATEMENT OF SUBJECT

10. INVESTIGATING OFFICERS	REPORT BY	11. DATE OF REPORT	12. APPROVED

F0680-79.2 (R5-90)

CASE NO. _____

SHERIFF'S DEPARTMENT
ORANGE COUNTY
SANTA ANA, CALIFORNIA

PRIORITY: ☐ YES
☐ NO

MICHAEL CARONA, SHERIFF-CORONER   **IN FIELD SHOW-UP REPORT**

OFFENSE	LOCATION OF OCCURRENCE	
VICTIM	DATE OF OCCURRENCE	GRID

ADMONITION OF VICTIMS AND WITNESSES:

It is requested that you look at an individual who has been temporarily detained by the Police. This person may or may not have committed the crime. It is just as important to eliminate an innocent person from suspicion, as it is to identify the person who committed the crime. You are under no obligation to identify this person. The fact that the person has been detained, may be handcuffed, seated in a Police car, or surrounded by Police Officers should not influence your decision. While viewing this individual, be aware of the possibility that the person being detained may have altered his/her appearance by using a disguise or by changing clothing since the time of the reported crime. The possibility should be considered in your final identification or elimination of the individual being detained. Please do not discuss the case with other witnesses or indicate in any way that you have or have not identified someone.

I fully understand the admonition presented to me by Officer _____,

regarding the In Field Show-Up. (Yes or No)_____.

(Signature of Witness)

IDENTIFICATION:

_____ I can not identify this individual as the suspect.

_____ I can identify this individual as the suspect.

ADDITIONAL COMMENTS OF VICTIM/WITNESSES:

_____

_____

_____

_____

_____

SIGNATURE OF WITNESS: _____ DATE: _____

WITNESSED BY OFFICER: _____ DATE/TIME: _____

LOCATION OF IN FLIELD SHOW-UP: _____

DATE & TIME OF IN FIELD SHOW-UP: _____

NAME AND DATE OF BIRTH OF PERSON VIEWED: _____

INVESTIGATING OFFICERS	REPORT BY	DATE OF REPORT	APPROVED

IN-FIELD SHOW-UP PROCEDURE

Even though <u>proper</u> In-Field Show-ups have been approved, a show-up which is impermissibly suggestive is still impermissible. To be sure your show-up identification will not be excluded at trial as unfair, follow these guidelines.

1. Take a detailed description of the suspect from the witness <u>before</u> the witness sees the detained suspect.

2. Read the Admonition Statement to the witness and have him sign the Admonition part of the report.

3. Transport the witness to the detained suspect's location.

4. Do not tell the witness any incriminating facts about the circumstances of the detention, such as --"We caught him running away", "He had your purse in his car", etc.

5. Do not offer any personal opinions about whether the detainee is, or is not, the perpetrator.

6. If safety permits, reduce the inherent suggestiveness by displaying the detainee outside the police car or without handcuffs.

7. If you have two or more witnesses, separate them <u>before</u> the show-up viewing, so they will be giving their independent opinion on the identification.

8. Display the detainee to the witness.

9. If possible, record the witness' exact words, such as, "That's him", "I think it's him", "I'm sure that's the guy."

10. Have the witness complete the identification and additional comments sections and sign and date the report.

11. The officer who witnessed the signature shall record the date and time of it.

12. Interview the witness about whether the suspect changed his clothing to disguise his appearance.

13. Display the weapon, vehicle or any stolen property to the witness for identification and record the witness' comments.

14. The officer shall complete the rest of the In-Field Show-Up report.

15. After the In-Field Show-Up, transport the witness back to his original location.

16. Be specific about your articulable suspicion to have detained the suspect for the show-up. Instead of saying, "He fit the description", say, "He was a white male in his twenties with dark hair, wearing blue coveralls, all as described in the dispatch or broadcast, and he was approximately 1/2 mile away from the scene and within fifteen minutes of the crime.

17. Book the original In-Field Show-Up report as evidence, and attach copies of it to your report.

CASE NO.

SHERIFF'S DEPARTMENT
ORANGE COUNTY
SANTA ANA, CALIFORNIA

PRIORITY: ☐ YES
☐ NO

MICHAEL S. CARONA, SHERIFF-CORONER

PHOTOGRAPHIC LINE-UP REPORT

OFFENSE	LOCATION OF OCCURRENCE	
VICTIM	DATE OF OCCURRENCE	GRID

PHOTOGRAPHIC LINE-UP:

On _____ (Date/Time), at _____ (location),
_____ (victim/witness's name) was read the following admonition, and
then allowed to view the photographic line-up.

ADMONITION OF VICTIMS AND WITNESSES:

It is requested that you look through a group of _____ photographs. You are under no obligation to pick out any photographs. The suspect(s) may or may not be in this photographic line-up. It is just as important to eliminate an innocent person from suspicion, as it is to identify the person who committed the crime. Take into consideration, that photographs may not depict what an individual looked like at the time of the offense. Therefore, special effort should be made to identify the suspect by physical characteristics. Please look at the photographs and to the best of your ability, see if you can identify any of the photographs as the suspect who committed the crime. Please do not discuss this case with any other possible witness, or indicate in any way that you have not identified someone.

I fully understand the admonition presented to me by Officer _____,
regarding the photographic line-up. (Yes or No) _____.
(Signature of Witness)

IDENTIFICATION:

_____ I can not make any identification.

_____ I can identify photograph #_____ as the suspect.

STATEMENT OF WITNESS/VICTIM:

_____

_____

_____

_____

_____

SIGNATURE OF WITNESS: _____ DATE: _____

WITNESSED BY OFFICER: _____ DATE/TIME: _____

PHOTOGRAPH # _____ IS THAT OF: _____

INVESTIGATING OFFICERS	REPORTED BY	DATE OF REPORT	APPROVED

F0680-353 (01/99)

PHOTOGRAPHIC LINEUP PROCEDURE

Even though <u>proper</u> Photographic Lineups have been approved, a line-up which is impermissibly suggestive is still impermissible. To be sure your lineup identification will not be excluded at trial as unfair, follow these guidelines.

1. The photographic lineup must consist of at least six (6) photographic.

2. If jail module mugs are to be used, be sure to remove them from the module cards.

3. Use all color <u>or</u> all black & white photographs, do not mix.

4. Everyone in the display should be of the same sex, race, approximate age and general features.

5. Try to use photographs of the same approximate size, depicting the same approximate shots of the faces such as all close ups or not close ups.

6. Arrange the six photographs in a Mug Show-up folder.

7. Label each photograph with a number from one (#1) through six (#6).

8. Record the identity of each person on the inside flap of the Mug Show-up folder.

9. Use a different Mug Show-up folder for each suspect, do not put two suspects in the same display.

10. If you have two or more witnesses, separate them <u>before</u> viewing the photographic lineup, so they will be giving their independent opinion on the identification.

11. Read the Admonition Statement to the witness and have him sign the Admonition part of the report.

12. Display the photographic lineup to the witness.

13. If possible, record the witness' exact words, such as, "That's him", "I think it's him", "I'm sure that's the guy."

14. Have the witness complete the identification and additional comments sections and sign and date the report.

15. If the witness can make an identification, be sure the photograph number of the suspect is entered on the report.

16. The officer who witnessed the signature shall record the date and time of it.

17. Interview the witness on whether the suspect's appearance is changed.

18. The officer shall complete the rest of the photographic lineup report.

19. Book the original photographic lineup report and the mug show-up folder as evidence, and attach copies of both to your report.

ASSIST OUTSIDE AGENCY
EXCEPTIONAL CLEARANCE ☐

SHERIFF-CORONER DEPARTMENT
ORANGE COUNTY
SANTA ANA, CALIFORNIA

CASE NO.
BKG. NO.
COURT JURISDICTION

MICHAEL S. CARONA, SHERIFF-CORONER

NARCOTIC/DRUG/INFLUENCE/USE REPORT

1. Offense		2. Location of Occurrence	3. Grid No.
4. Name		5. AKA	
6. Address		7. Date of Birth	8. Place of Birth

9. Sex	Race	Age	Ht.	Wt.	Hair	Eyes	10. Occupation

11. Any Recent Injuries?		Doctor	When

12. Any Recent Illnesses?	Glaucoma	Diabetes	Syphillis	Donated Blood	When	What

13. Advisement of Rights
You have the right to remain silent. ("Do you understand?")
Anything you say may be used against you in court. ("Do you understand?")
You have the right to an attorney before and during any questioning. ("Do you understand?")
If you can not afford an attorney, one will be appointed for you before questioning, if you wish. ("Do you understand that?")
Expressed waiver: Can we talk about what happened?

Given by: Time:

14. When did you fix last?	15. Type of Syringe	16. Self Injected	17. Where on body	18. What
19. Examination Location	20. Room Light Condition		21. Mechanical Aids used	

22. Pupils Reaction to Light ☐ Nose ☐ Slight ☐ Hipus ☐ Normal	Remarks
23. Pupilary Appearance ☐ Constricted ☐ Normal ☐ Dilated	
24. Somnolence ☐ Heavy ☐ Moderate ☐ Slight ☐ None Noted	
25. Eyelid Appearance ☐ Closing ☐ Drooping ☐ Heavy ☐ Normal	
26. Rubbing of Face ☐ Heavy ☐ Moderate ☐ Slight ☐ None	
27. Scratching of Body ☐ Heavy ☐ Moderate ☐ Slight ☐ None	

28. Alcohol Odor	Dry Mouth	Blood Obtained By	Vial No.	Location	Time	Arm
29. Photos	Photographer	Where	What	Time	Witnesses	

30. Additional Comments:

31. Investigation Officer	Reported By	32. Date of Report	33. Approved

SHF 037 (05-99)

34. Description of Clothing

35. Description of Marks: Right Side	36. Description of Marks: Left Side

37. Tie Off Bruises Noted	38. Where

39. Location of Marks: Right Side	40. Location of Mark: Left Side

41. Conclusions

LEFT THUMB

RIGHT THUMB

42. Investigating Officers	43. Date

APPLICATION FOR EMERGENCY PROTECTIVE ORDER (CLETS)   1295.90

(Name): _____ has provided the information in items 1-5.

LAW ENFORCEMENT CASE NUMBER:

1. PERSON(S) TO BE PROTECTED *(insert names of all persons to be protected by this order)*:

_____

_____

2. PERSON TO BE RESTRAINED *(name)*: _____

Sex: ☐ M ☐ F Ht.:_____ Wt.:_____ Hair color:____ Eye color:____ Race:_____ Age:____ Date of birth:_____

3. The events that cause the protected person to fear immediate and present danger of domestic violence, child abuse, child abduction, elder or dependent adult abuse, or stalking (including workplace violence or civil harassment) are *(give facts and dates; specify weapons)*: _____

_____

_____

_____

4. ☐ The person to be protected lives with the person to be restrained and requests an order that the restrained person move out immediately from the address in item 9.

5. a. ☐ The person to be protected has minor children in common with the person to be restrained, and a temporary custody order is requested because of the facts alleged in item 3. A custody order ☐ does ☐ does not exist.

   b. ☐ The person to be protected is a minor child in immediate danger of being abducted by the person to be restrained because of the facts alleged in item 3.

6. ☐ A child welfare worker or probation officer has advised the undersigned that a juvenile court petition
   ☐ will be filed.   ☐ will NOT be filed.

7. ☐ Adult Protective Services has been notified.

8. Phone call to *(name of judicial officer)*: _____ on *(date)*:_____ at *(time)*:_____
   ☐ The judicial officer granted the **Emergency Protective Order** that follows.

By: _____   ▶ _____
      (PRINT NAME OF LAW ENFORCEMENT OFFICER)   (SIGNATURE OF LAW ENFORCEMENT OFFICER)

Agency: _____ Telephone No.: _____ Badge No.: _____

EMERGENCY PROTECTIVE ORDER

9. To restrained person *(name)*: _____

   a. ☐ You must not contact, molest, harass, attack, strike, threaten, sexually assault, batter, telephone, send any messages to, follow, stalk, destroy any personal property, or disturb the peace of each person named in item 1.

   b. ☐ You must ☐ stay away at least _____ yards from each person named in item 1.
                  ☐ stay away at least _____ yards from ☐ move out immediately from

      (address): _____

10. ☐ *(Name)*: _____ is given temporary care and control of the following minor children of the parties *(names and ages)*: _____

_____

11. Reasonable grounds for the issuance of this order exist and an emergency protective order is necessary to prevent the occurrence or recurrence of domestic violence, child abuse, child abduction, elder or dependent adult abuse, or stalking (including workplace violence or civil harassment).

12. **THIS EMERGENCY PROTECTIVE ORDER WILL EXPIRE AT 5:00 P.M. ON:**

    To protected person: If you need protection for a longer period of time, you must request permanent protective orders at *(court name and address)*:

INSERT DATE OF FIFTH COURT DAY OR SEVENTH CALENDAR DAY, WHICHEVER IS EARLIER; DO NOT COUNT DAY THE ORDER IS GRANTED

PROOF OF SERVICE

13. Person served *(name)*: _____

14. I personally delivered copies to the person served as follows: Date: _____ Time: _____
    Address: _____

15. At the time of service I was at least 18 years of age and not a party to this cause.

16. My name, address, and telephone number are *(this does not have to be server's home telephone number or address)*:

_____

☐ California sheriff or marshal

I declare under penalty of perjury under the laws of the State of California that the foregoing is true and correct.

Date: _____   ▶

_____ *(See reverse for important notices)* _____
(TYPE OR PRINT NAME OF SERVER)   (SIGNATURE OF SERVER)

Form Adopted for Mandatory Use
Judicial Council of California
1295.90 [Rev. January 1, 2000]
Approved by DOJ

EMERGENCY PROTECTIVE ORDER (CLETS)
(Domestic Violence, Child Abuse, Elder or Dependent
Adult Abuse, Workplace Violence, Civil Harassment)
ONE copy to court, ONE copy to restrained person, ONE copy to protected person, ONE copy to issuing agency

Family Code, § 6240 et seq.
Penal Code, § 646.91

EMERGENCY PROTECTIVE ORDER
WARNINGS AND INFORMATION

VIOLATION OF THIS ORDER IS A MISDEMEANOR PUNISHABLE BY A $1,000 FINE, ONE YEAR IN JAIL, OR BOTH, OR MAY BE PUNISHABLE AS A FELONY. PENAL CODE SECTION 12021(g) PROHIBITS ANY PERSON SUBJECT TO A RESTRAINING ORDER FROM PURCHASING OR ATTEMPTING TO PURCHASE OR OTHERWISE OBTAIN A FIREARM. SUCH CONDUCT IS SUBJECT TO A $1,000 FINE AND IMPRISONMENT OR BOTH. THIS ORDER SHALL BE ENFORCED BY ALL LAW ENFORCEMENT OFFICERS IN THE STATE OF CALIFORNIA WHO ARE AWARE OF OR SHOWN A COPY OF THE ORDER. UNDER PENAL CODE SECTION 13710(b), "THE TERMS AND CONDITIONS OF THE PROTECTION ORDER REMAIN ENFORCEABLE, NOTWITHSTANDING THE ACTS OF THE PARTIES, AND MAY BE CHANGED ONLY BY ORDER OF THE COURT."

To the restrained person: This order will last until the date and time in item 12 on the reverse. The protected person may, however, obtain a more permanent restraining order when the court opens. You may seek the advice of an attorney as to any matter connected with this order. The attorney should be consulted promptly so that the attorney may assist you in responding to the order.

A la persona bajo restricción judicial: Esta orden durará hasta la fecha y hora indicadas en el punto 12 al dorso. La persona protegida puede, sin embargo, obtener una Orden de entredicho (restricción judicial) más permanente cuando la corte abra. Usted puede consultar a un abogado en conexión con cualquier asunto relacionado con esta orden. Debe consultar al abogado sin pérdida de tiempo para que él o ella le pueda ayudar a responder a la orden.

To the protected person: This order will last only until the date and time noted in item 12 on the reverse. If you wish to seek continuing protection, you will have to apply for an order from the court at the address on the reverse, when it opens, or you should apply to the court in the county where you live if it is a different county and the violence is likely to occur there. You may apply for a protective order free of charge. In the case of an endangered child, you may also apply for a more permanent order at the address on the reverse, or if there is a juvenile dependency action pending you may apply for a more permanent order under section 213.5 of the Welfare and Institutions Code. In the case of a child being abducted, you may apply for a *Child Custody Order* from the court at the address on the reverse side of this form. You may seek the advice of an attorney as to any matter connected with your application for any future court orders. The attorney should be consulted promptly so that the attorney may assist you in making your application. You do not have to have an attorney to get the protective order.

A la persona protegida: Esta orden durará sólo hasta la fecha y hora indicadas en el punto 12 al dorso. Si usted desea que la protección continúe, tendrá que solicitar una orden de la corte en la dirección indicada al dorso cuando la corte abra, o tendrá que hacer la solicitud ante la corte del condado donde usted vive, si se trata de un condado diferente y es probable que la violencia ocurra allí. La solicitud de la orden de protección es gratis. En el caso de que un niño o una niña se encuentre en peligro, puede solicitar una orden más permanente en la dirección indicada al dorso o, si hay una acción legal pendiente de tutela juvenil, puede solicitar una orden más permanente conforme a la sección 213.5 del código titulado en inglés **Welfare and Institutions Code.** En el caso del secuestro de un niño o una niña, usted puede solicitar de la corte una Orden para la guarda del niño o de la niña *(Child Custody Order)*, en la dirección indicada al dorso de este formulario. Puede consultar a un abogado en conexión con cualquier asunto relacionado con las solicitudes de órdenes de la corte que usted presente en el futuro. Debe consultar un abogado sin perdida de tiempo para que él o ella le pueda ayudar a presentar su solicitud. Para obtener la orden de protección no es necesario que un abogado le represente.

To law enforcement: Penal Code section 13710(c) provides that, upon request, law enforcement shall serve the party to be restrained at the scene of a domestic violence incident or at any time the restrained party is in custody. The officer who requested the emergency protective order, while on duty, shall carry copies of the order. The emergency protective order shall be served upon the restrained party by the officer, if the restrained party can reasonably be located, and a copy shall be given to the protected party. A copy also shall be filed with the court as soon as practicable after issuance. The availability of an emergency protective order shall not be affected by the fact that the endangered person has vacated the household to avoid abuse. A law enforcement officer shall use every reasonable means to enforce an emergency protective order issued pursuant to this subdivision. A law enforcement officer acting pursuant to this subdivision shall not be held civilly or criminally liable if he or she has acted in good faith with regard thereto.

If a child is in danger of being abducted: This order will last only until the date and time noted in the *Emergency Protective Order.* You may apply for a child custody order from the court, on the reverse side of this form.

En el caso de peligro de secuestro de un niño o de una niña: Esta orden será válida sólo hasta la hora y fecha indicadas en la Orden de protección de emergencia *(Emergency Protective Order).* Usted puede solicitar de la corte una Orden para la guarda del niño o de la niña *(Child Custody Order),* en la dirección indicada al dorso.

This emergency protective order is effective when made. This order shall expire not later than the close of judicial business on the fifth day of judicial business following the day of its issue. An emergency protective order is also available to prevent the occurrence of child abuse.

1295.90 [Rev. January 1, 2000]

EMERGENCY PROTECTIVE ORDER (CLETS)
(Domestic Violence, Child Abuse, Elder or Dependent
Adult Abuse, Workplace Violence, Civil Harassment)
ONE copy to court, ONE copy to restrained person, ONE copy to protected person, ONE copy to issuing agency

Page two

ORANGE COUNTY SHERIFF'S DEPARTMENT — DOMESTIC VIOLENCE SUPPLEMENTAL 13700 P.C.

VICTIM'S NAME (L, F, M)	DATE OF BIRTH	CASE NUMBER	OFFENSE

I responded to a call of _____ at _____

I found the victim _____

ORIGIN / CRIME DESCRIPTION

VICTIM

The victim displayed the following emotional and physical conditions:

- [ ] ANGRY
- [ ] APOLOGETIC
- [ ] CRYING
- [ ] FEARFUL
- [ ] HYSTERICAL
- [ ] CALM
- [ ] AFRAID
- [ ] IRRATIONAL
- [ ] NERVOUS
- [ ] THREATENING
- [ ] OTHER: EXPLAIN

- [ ] COMP OF PAIN
- [ ] BRUISE(S)
- [ ] ABRASION(S)
- [ ] MINOR CUT(S)
- [ ] LACERATION(S)
- [ ] FRACTURE(S)
- [ ] CONCUSSION(S)
- [ ] OTHER: EXPLAIN

ALWAYS explain OPPOSITES in narrative.

SUSPECT

- [ ] ANGRY
- [ ] APOLOGETIC
- [ ] CRYING
- [ ] FEARFUL
- [ ] HYSTERICAL
- [ ] CALM
- [ ] AFRAID
- [ ] IRRATIONAL
- [ ] NERVOUS
- [ ] THREATENING
- [ ] OTHER: EXPLAIN

- [ ] COMP OF PAIN
- [ ] BRUISE(S)
- [ ] ABRASION(S)
- [ ] MINOR CUT(S)
- [ ] LACERATION(S)
- [ ] FRACTURE(S)
- [ ] CONCUSSION(S)
- [ ] OTHER: EXPLAIN

ALWAYS explain OPPOSITES in narrative.

- [ ] CONTINUED

SUSPECT'S NAME	DATE OF BIRTH
HOME ADDRESS	TELEPHONE
WORK ADDRESS	TELEPHONE

RELATIONSHIP BETWEEN VICTIM AND SUSPECT
MARK ALL THAT APPLY

- [ ] SPOUSE
- [ ] FORMER SPOUSE
- [ ] COHABITANTS
- [ ] FORMER COHABITANTS
- [ ] DATING/ENGAGED
- [ ] FORMER DATING
- [ ] SAME SEX
- [ ] EMANCIPATED MINOR
- [ ] PARENT OF CHILD FROM RELATIONSHIP

LENGTH OF RELATIONSHIP

_____ YEAR(s) _____ MONTH(s)

IF APPLICABLE,
DATE RELATIONSHIP ENDED: _____

PRIOR HISTORY OF DOMESTIC VIOLENCE? [ ] YES [ ] NO
PRIOR HISTORY OF VIOLENCE DOCUMENTED? [ ] YES [ ] NO

NUMBER OF PRIOR INCIDENTS: [ ] MINOR [ ] SERIOUS

CASE NUMBER (s) _____

INVESTIGATING AGENCY: _____

MEDICAL TREATMENT

- [ ] NONE
- [ ] WILL SEEK OWN DOCTOR
- [ ] FIRST AID
- [ ] PARAMEDICS
- [ ] HOSPITAL
- [ ] REFUSED MEDICAL AID

PARAMEDICS AT SCENE: [ ] YES [ ] NO

UNIT NUMBER: _____
NAME(S) ID#: _____

HOSPITAL: _____

ATTENDING PHYSICIAN (s): _____

EVIDENCE

EVIDENCE COLLECTED:

FROM: [ ] Crime Scene [ ] Hospital [ ] Other: Explain

PHOTOS: [ ] Yes [ ] No   Number: _____

TYPE: [ ] 35mm [ ] Polaroid

TAKEN BY: _____

DESCRIBE ALL PHOTOGRAPHS

Photos of victim's injuries: [ ] Yes [ ] No
Photos of suspect's injuries: [ ] Yes [ ] No
Weapon used during incident [ ] Yes [ ] No

Type of weapon used: _____
Weapon(s) impounded: [ ] Yes [ ] No
Firearm(s) impounded for safety: [ ] Yes [ ] No

EVIDENCE BOOKED AT: _____

DESCRIBE ALL EVIDENCE AND DISPOSITION

REPORTING OFFICER	ID NUMBER	DATE & TIME	APPROVED BY:

WITNESSES			
WITNESSES PRESENT DURING DOMESTIC VIOLENCE?	☐ YES	☐ NO	
STATEMENT(S) TAKEN?	☐ YES	☐ NO	
CHILDREN PRESENT DURING DOMESTIC VIOLENCE?	☐ YES	☐ NO	NUMBER PRESENT ___ AGE(S) ___
STATEMENT(S)?	☐ YES	☐ NO	

RESTRAINING ORDERS: ☐ YES ☐ NO
☐ CURRENT ☐ EXPIRED
TYPE: ☐ EMERGENCY ☐ TEMPORARY ☐ PERMANENT

ISSUING COURT: _____

ORDER OR DOCKET NUMBER: _____

VICTIM GIVEN:

☐ DOMESTIC VIOLENCE INFORMATION SHEET

☐ OCSD CASE NUMBER

☐ DOMESTIC VIOLENCE UNIT PHONE NUMBER

IS THE VICTIM AT A TEMPORARY ADDRESS? ☐ Y/N.   If YES, attach a **memo** with the address and phone number.

V.   S. (Circle One)

HT. _____

WT. _____

PLEASE DRAW ON DIAGRAMS(S) THE LOCATION OF ANY INJURIES.

V.   S. (Circle One)

HT. _____

WT. _____

SUSPECTED CHILD ABUSE REPORT
To Be Completed by Reporting Party
Pursuant to Penal Code Section 11166

A. CASE IDENTIFICATION

TO BE COMPLETED BY INVESTIGATING CPA

VICTIM NAME: _____

REPORT NO./CASE NAME: _____

DATE OF REPORT: _____

B. REPORTING PARTY

NAME/TITLE

ADDRESS

PHONE ( )   DATE OF REPORT   SIGNATURE

C. REPORT SENT TO

☐ POLICE DEPARTMENT   ☐ SHERIFF'S OFFICE   ☐ COUNTY WELFARE   ☐ COUNTY PROBATION

AGENCY   ADDRESS

OFFICIAL CONTACTED   PHONE ( )   DATE/TIME

D. INVOLVED PARTIES

VICTIM

NAME (LAST, FIRST, MIDDLE)	ADDRESS	BIRTHDATE	SEX	RACE

PRESENT LOCATION OF CHILD   PHONE ( )

SIBLINGS

	NAME	BIRTHDATE	SEX	RACE		NAME	BIRTHDATE	SEX	RACE
1.					4.				
2.					5.				
3.					6.				

PARENTS

NAME (LAST, FIRST, MIDDLE)	BIRTHDATE	SEX	RACE	NAME (LAST, FIRST, MIDDLE)	BIRTHDATE	SEX	RACE

| ADDRESS | | | | ADDRESS | | | |

| HOME PHONE ( ) | BUSINESS PHONE ( ) | | | HOME PHONE ( ) | BUSINESS PHONE ( ) | | |

E. INCIDENT INFORMATION

IF NECESSARY, ATTACH EXTRA SHEET OR OTHER FORM AND CHECK THIS BOX. ☐

1. DATE/TIME OF INCIDENT   PLACE OF INCIDENT   *(CHECK ONE)*   ☐ OCCURRED   ☐ OBSERVED

IF CHILD WAS IN OUT-OF-HOME CARE AT TIME OF INCIDENT, CHECK TYPE OF CARE.

☐ FAMILY DAY CARE   ☐ CHILD CARE CENTER   ☐ FOSTER FAMILY HOME   ☐ SMALL FAMILY HOME   ☐ GROUP HOME OR INSTITUTION

2. TYPE OF ABUSE: *(CHECK ONE OR MORE)*   ☐ PHYSICAL   ☐ MENTAL   ☐ SEXUAL ASSAULT   ☐ NEGLECT   ☐ OTHER

3. NARRATIVE DESCRIPTION:

4. SUMMARIZE WHAT THE ABUSED CHILD OR PERSON ACCOMPANYING THE CHILD SAID HAPPENED:

5. EXPLAIN KNOWN HISTORY OF SIMILAR INCIDENT(S) FOR THIS CHILD:

SS 8572 (Rev. 1/93)

INSTRUCTIONS AND DISTRIBUTION ON REVERSE

DO NOT submit a copy of this form to the Department of Justice (DOJ). A CPA is required under Penal Code Section 11169 to submit to DOJ a Child Abuse Investigation Report Form SS-8583 if (1) an active investigation has been conducted and (2) the incident is **not** unfounded.

Police or Sheriff-WHITE Copy; County Welfare or Probation-BLUE Copy; District Attorney-GREEN Copy; Reporting Party-YELLOW Copy

DEFINITIONS AND GENERAL INSTRUCTIONS FOR COMPLETION OF FORM SS 8572

I. REPORTING RESPONSIBILITIES

- No child care custodian or health practitioner or commercial film and photographic print processor reporting a suspected instance of child abuse shall be civilly or ciminally liable for any report required or authorized by this article (California Penal Code Article 2.5). Any other person reporting a suspected instance of child abuse shall not incur civil or ciminal liability as a result of any report authorized by this section unless it can be proved that a false report was made and the person knew or should have known that the report was false.

- Any child care custodian, health practitioner, commercial film and photographic print processor, or employee of a child protective agency who has knowledge of or observes a child in his or her professional capacity or within the scope of his or her employment whom he or she reasonably suspects has been the victim of child abuse shall report such suspected instance of child abuse to a child protective agency immediately or as soon as practically possible by telephone and shall prepare and send a written report thereof *within 36 hours* of receiving the information concerning the incident.

- Any child care custodian, health practitioner, commercial film and photographic print processor, or employee of a child protective agency who has knowledge of or who reasonably suspects that mental suffering has been inflicted on a child or its emotional well-being is endangered in any other way, may report such suspected instance of child abuse to a child protective agency. Infliction of willful and unjustifiable mental suffering must be reported.

II. DEFINITIONS

- "Child care custodian" means a teacher; an instructional aide, a teacher's aide, or a teacher's assistant employed by any public or private school, who has been trained in the duties imposed by this article, if the school district has so warranted to the State Department of Education; a classified employee of any public school who has been trained in the duties imposed by this article, if the school has so warranted to the State Department of Education; an administrative officer, supervisor of child welfare and attendance, or certificated pupil personnel employee of any public or private school; an administrator of a public or private day camp; an administrator or employee of a public or private youth center, youth recreation program, or youth organization; an administrator or employee of a public or private organization whose duties require direct contact and supervision of children; a licensee, an administrator, or an employee of a licensed community care or child day care facility; a headstart teacher; a licensing worker or licensing evaluator; a public assistance worker; an employee of a child care institution including, but not limited to, foster parents, group home personnel, and personnel of residential care facilities; a social worker, probation officer, or parole officer; an employee of a school district police or security department; any person who is an administrator or presenter of, or a counselor in, a child abuse prevention program in any public or private school; a district attorney investigator, inspector, or family support officer unless the investigator, inspector, or officer is working with an attorney appointed pursuant to Section 317 of the Welfare and Institutions Code to represent a minor; or a peace officer, as defined in Chapter 4.5 (commencing with Section 830) of Title 3 of Part 2 of this code, who is not otherwise described in this section.

- "Health practitioner" means a physician and surgeon, psychiatrist, psychologist, dentist, resident, intern, podiatrist, chiropractor, licensed nurse, dental hygienist, optometrist, or any other person who is currently licensed under Division 2 (commencing with Section 500) of the Business and Professions Code; a marriage, family and child counselor; any emergency medical technician I or II, paramedic, or other person certified pursuant to Division 2.5 (commencing with Section 1797) of the Health and Safety Code; a psychological assistant registered pursuant to Section 2913 of the Business and Professions Code; a marriage, family and child counselor trainee, as defined in subdivision (c) of Section 4980.03 of the Business and Professions Code; an unlicensed marriage, family and child counselor intern registered under Section 4980.44 of the Business and Professions Code; a state or county public health employee who treats a minor for venereal disease or any other condition; a coroner; a medical examiner, or any other person who performs autopsies; or a religious practitioner who diagnoses, examines, or treats children.

- "Commercial film and photographic print processor" means any person who develops exposed photographic film into negatives, slides, or prints, or who makes prints from negatives or slides, for compensation. The term includes any employee of such a person; it does not include a person who develops film or makes prints for a public agency.

- "Child protective agency" means a police or sheriff's department, a county probation department, or a county welfare department. It does not include a school district police or security department.

III. INSTRUCTIONS

(Section A to be completed by investigating child protective agency)
SECTION A - "CASE IDENTIFICATION": Enter the victim name, report number or case name, and date of report.

(Sections B through E are to be completed by reporting party)
SECTION B - "REPORTING PARTY": Enter your name/title, address, phone number, date of report, and signature.

SECTION C - "REPORT SENT TO": (1) Check the appropriate box to indicate which child protective agency (CPA) this report is being sent; (2) Enter the name and address of the CPA to which this report is being sent; and (3) Enter the name of the official contacted at the CPA, phone number, and the date/time contacted.

SECTION D - "INVOLVED PARTIES":

a. VICTIM: Enter the name, address, physical data, present location, and phone number where victim is located (attach additional sheets if multiple victims).

b. SIBLINGS: Enter the name and physical data of siblings living in the same household as the victim.

c. PARENTS: Enter the names, physical data, addresses, and phone numbers of father/stepfather and mother/stepmother.

SECTION E - "INCIDENT INFORMATION": (1) Enter the date/ time and place the incident occurred or was observed, and check the appropriate boxes; (2) Check the type of abuse; (3) Describe injury or sexual assault (where appropriate, attach Medical Report - Suspected Child Abuse Form DOJ 900 or any other form desired); (4) Summarize what the child or person accompanying the child said happened; and (5) Explain any known prior incidents involving the victim.

IV. DISTRIBUTION

A. Reporting Party: Complete Suspected Child Abuse Report Form SS 8572. Retain yellow copy for your records and submit top three copies to a child protective agency.

B. Investigating Child Protective Agency: Upon receipt of Form SS 8572, *within 36 hours* send white copy to police or sheriff, blue copy to county welfare or probation, and green copy to district attorney.

PRELIMINARY INVESTIGATION GUIDE

A good preliminary investigation will discover answers to nine questions:

1. *What*: The type of incident that happened.
2. *Who*: All persons that were involved in the incident.
3. *When:* The date and time the incident happened.
4. *Where:* The address where the incident happened.
5. *Vehicle:* All vehicles that were involved in the incident.
6. *Property:* All property that was involved in the incident.
7. *How:* A paragraph that tells step by step how the incident happened.
8. *Why:* A paragraph that tells why the incident happened.
9. *Other Information:* A paragraph of information that completes the report.

Gather information for your report by using the word PRELIMINARY:

Step 1:		Probable cause to begin the PRELIMINARY investigation.
Step 2:	P	Proceed to the scene of the incident.
Step 3:	R	Render aid to the victim.
Step 4:	E	Effect the arrest of the suspect if possible.
Step 5:	L	Locate witnesses of the incident.
Step 6:	I	Interview witnesses of the incident.
Step 7:	M	Maintain the crime scene in its original condition.
Step 8:	I	Interrogate the suspect of the crime if appropriate.
Step 9:	N	Note all PRELIMINARY investigation findings.
Step 10:	A	Arrange for the crime lab to process the crime scene.

Step 11:	R	Report to be written.
Step 12:	Y	Yield to the follow-up investigators when appropriate.
Step 13:		Improving your PRELIMINARY investigations skills.

Here's a complete explanation for each of the 13 steps in a PRELIMINARY investigation.

Step 1—Have Probable Cause to Begin Your Preliminary Investigation

1. Probable cause may include:
   a. Communications sends you an assignment,
   b. Someone flags you down,
   c. You see something wrong,
   d. You smell something wrong,
   e. You hear something wrong, or
   f. You know something is wrong.

2. Once you have probable cause to begin a preliminary investigation, the PRELIMINARY spells out how to complete the investigation.
3. Memorize the word PRELIMINARY, and memorize what each letter in the word stands for. Then follow the PRELIMINARY steps to handle every incident.
4. Clearly note in your notebook and report every relevant thing you find as you take the PRELIMINARY steps.

Step 2—Proceed to the Scene

1. As quickly and safely as possible, but above all else get there.
2. Keep your eyes open for persons and vehicles as you come onto the scene.
3. Ask yourself, "What happened here?"
4. Quickly plan what you are going to do, so you will be ready for whatever you find at the scene.
5. Clearly show in your report the relevant things you found when you went to the scene and arrived at the incident.

Step 3—Render Aid

1. Saving life is first, before you begin taking any other PRELIMINARY investigation steps.
2. Clearly show in your report the injury or damage you saw and the assistance you or others gave.

Step 4—Effect the Arrest

1. When you see the suspect do the crime.
2. If you can when the victim or witness tells you they saw the suspect do the crime.
3. Search the suspect for weapons.
4. Have the victim or witness sign the private person arrest form if appropriate.

5. Immediately give communications a suspect and/or vehicle description and direction of travel.
6. Clearly show in your report your probable cause to stop, detain, arrest, and search.
7. Clearly show in your report the actions you took and whatever your search found.

Step 5—Locate All Witnesses

1. By looking for them, asking around, canvasing, and knocking on doors.
2. Separate them so they can't discuss the incident among themselves.
3. List all witnesses in your report.

Step 6—Interview All Witnesses and Ask

1. What happened, so you can learn what to title your report.
2. When it happened, so you can learn the date and time the incident happened.
3. Where it happened, so you learn the address and jurisdiction where it happened.
4. Who they are, so you can reach them later.
5. Description of the suspect, so you can catch who did it.
6. Description of the suspect's vehicle.
7. Description of property taken.
8. Them to tell you step-by-step what they saw the suspect do.
9. Them if they know why the suspect committed the crime.
10. Clearly show in your report the answers the witness(s) gave you.

Step 7—Maintain the Crime Scene

1. By finding out the boundaries of the crime scene.
2. By letting no one enter the boundaries of the crime scene.
3. Clearly show in your report the condition of the crime scene.

Step 8 Interrogate the Suspect—Based on Current Statutory and Case Law

1. If appropriate by telling the suspect his Miranda rights, and then,
2. If the suspect understands and waives his Miranda rights, ask pertinent questions about the crime.
3. Clearly show in your report that you gave the Miranda warning, and whatever responses the suspect made to the Miranda warning.

Step 9—Note All Findings

1. By writing all your PRELIMINARY investigation findings in your notebook.
2. Then by writing those findings in your report narrative.

Step 10—Arrange for the Crime Lab or Crime Scene Investigation (CSI)

1. By following department policy for those notifications.
2. Clearly show in your report the date, time, name, and identification number of whom you notified to process the crime scene.

Step 11—Report Is to Be Written

1. Make sure you have done a complete PRELIMIINARY investigation before you begin writing your report.
2. Make sure you organize chronologically the information in mind and on your notepad before you start writing your report.
3. Make sure you complete all required "boxes" or blanks on the report form.
4. Make sure you complete the narrative.
5. Make sure you use the proper report writing mechanics.

Step 12—Yield to the Follow-Up Investigators

1. The investigators read your report and retrace your PRELIMINARY investigation steps.
2. The prosecuting attorney reads your report and retraces your PRELIMINARY investigation to see if you gave them enough information to prosecute the suspect.
3. The defense attorney reads your report and retraces your PRELIMINARY investigation to see if there is a flaw that will show a jury there is a reasonable doubt that the suspect is guilty.
4. You reread the report and retrace your PRELIMINARY investigation steps before you go to court to testify.

Step 13—Improving Your PRELIMINARY Investigation Skills

1. If the judge or jury finds the suspect not guilty, find out what went wrong and don't let it happen again.
2. It is the PRELIMINARY investigator's chief responsibility to get the skills necessary to put a prosecutable case together.
3. Talk to experts and read the experts who have a proven record of successful prosecutions. Keep alert, and don't let anything slip past you unnoticed.

Index